# THE COMING OF THE COMFORTER

# The COMING of the
# COMFORTER

By
**LE ROY EDWIN FROOM**

*Revised Edition*

REVIEW AND HERALD® PUBLISHING ASSOCIATION
HAGERSTOWN, MD 21740

# DEDICATION

*To the Gospel Ministry of the*
*Advent Movement, Who, Through*
*the Enabling Power of the Holy*
*Spirit in the Latter Rain, Are*
*Destined to Be the Instrumen-*
*talities for Finishing Our Com-*
*missioned World Task, This Vol-*
*ume Is Prayerfully Inscribed*

# CONTENTS

# *Spirit of Life*

LOVELY as bright sunshine after rain,
  When birds sing blithe and gay;
Cool, refreshing as a mountain spring,
  When faint, at heat of day;

Richer than the cherry's tapestry
  Of pink against the blue;
Sweeter than love's tender lullaby—
  Thy presence, Spirit true.

Precious Thy infilling, Spirit pure,
  For Thou dost life impart.
Overflow my little cup, but first,
  O fill my thirsting heart!
                    —ALFONSO N. ANDERSON.

*By Way of*

# INTRODUCTION

≪≪≪≪≪≪

THE studies on the Holy Spirit, comprising this volume, were first presented to the delegates and workers of the quadrennial ministerial institutes held in conjunction with the union conference sessions in the spring of 1928. The gracious presence of the Holy Spirit in these gatherings and presentations is most gratefully remembered, and reverent acknowledgment given therefor to our heavenly Father.

At the urgent request of hundreds of ministers present when this matter was orally delivered, these studies are here placed in permanent and accessible form.

And by request, the introductory remarks preceding the presentations are reproduced as accurately as memory will permit, so that the entire setting may be as nearly identical as possible.

\*   \*   \*

A most solemn sense of responsibility rests upon me as I contemplate the hours we are to spend together in earnest, searching study. A sobering consciousness of accountability to God overshadows all other considerations. Frankly, I did not choose this line of study. The constraint of a great pressure has for months rested down upon me—a conviction that I could not cast off, leading along in the research. I am profoundly convinced that God has led me to sense my own need, and the need of my fellow workers. This has led to a mighty outcry in my own soul for the one adequate provision for our common needs. And I pray that these studies may prove a genuine blessing and help, however faultily and inadequately they are presented.

We have not gathered to hear one another preach, however proper that may be. Nor are we here to be entertained by clever, original turn of thought nor to indulge in speculative theory. Rather, we have assembled for deep, sober study, and for earnest, intensive search after *great truths, mighty principles,* and *adequate provisions* commensurate with an hour like this.

It is foundationally necessary to understand certain factors at the outset. We live in a rapidly changing world—a world running riot with new forces. Wild passions loosed from the pit have produced a new world situation during the last decade or so. Humanity does not understand the malign influences that are driving the race away from God in indifference, defiance, and rebellion. And the situation is intensifying and complicating with each passing year.

New and grave problems, springing from a new and sinister attitude of mind and heart toward God and divine authority, confront and challenge us. We are passing through a transition period from sober, serious, reverent thought to light, trifling, and defiling amusement. It is my conviction that men and women are harder to reach with our redemptive gospel message than they were even a few years ago.

The tremendous cities of the world, yearly growing bigger, confront us with a staggering task. Within a radius of 135 miles of Springfield, Mass., where the Atlantic Union ministerial institute was held, a population of 13,000,000 reside; while within a radius of 100 miles of New York's City Hall 20,000,000 souls are said to live. Similar totals could be assembled elsewhere. And we are scarcely touching the citadels of men, women, and children with the tips of our fingers. Yet they must hear God's message to men.

The battle with evil forces constantly grows sharper and more sinister. I am persuaded that there is only one solution to the problem we face individually and denominationally, one provision for our need—and that is the power of the Holy Spirit, the outpouring of the latter rain in our lives and service. This promised provision falling upon the heralds of Heaven's last message to earth is our supreme necessity. This alone will enable us to cope with this stupendous situation and to finish the work committed to us. I have believed this for years, but somehow it had never gripped me so intensely before. I pray that this same divine compulsion may grip each evangelistic worker of the Advent Movement.

In preparation for these studies, following a close survey of every text in the Bible on the Holy Spirit, I read every reference thereto in the twenty-three volumes of the Spirit of prophecy, as well as many articles appearing in the past in our denominational journals from the pen of Mrs. E. G. White, and many testimonies still in manuscript. From this encompassing array of material the outstanding statements and principles were selected. (They appear scattered through the studies.) These were taken as the guide and norm in studying further some fifty volumes on the Holy Spirit representing the choicest gems written in modern times, and scanning many more as collateral reading. Thus were formed the three divisions of this volume on the *Promise,* the *Coming,* and the *Filling* of the Spirit.

\*          \*          \*

Before approaching the studies, the reader is asked to ponder carefully and prayerfully the two extracts which follow:

"The promise of the Spirit is a matter little thought of; and the result is only what might be expected,—spiritual drought, spiritual darkness, spiritual declension and death. Minor matters occupy the attention, and the divine power which is necessary for the growth and prosperity of the church, and which would bring all other blessings in its train, is lacking, though offered in its infinite plenitude."— *Testimonies,* vol. 8, p. 21.

"Just prior to His leaving His disciples for the heavenly courts, Jesus encouraged them with the promise of the Holy Spirit. This promise belongs as much to us as it did to them, and *yet how rarely it is presented before the people, and its reception spoken of in the church.* In consequence of this *silence* upon this most important theme, what promise do we know less about by its practical fulfillment than this rich promise of the gift of the Holy Spirit, whereby efficiency is to be given to all our spiritual labor? The promise of the Holy Spirit is *casually* brought into our discourses, is *incidentally* touched upon, and that is all. Prophecies have been dwelt upon, doctrines have been expounded; but that which is essential to the church in order that they may grow in spiritual strength and efficiency, in order that the preaching may carry conviction with it, and souls be converted to God, *has been largely left out* of ministerial effort. This subject has been set aside, as if some time in the future would be given to its consideration. Other blessings and privileges have been presented before the people until a desire has been awakened in the church for the attainment of the blessing promised of God; *but the impression concerning the Holy Spirit has been that this gift is not for the church now, but*

*that at some time in the future it would be necessary
for the church to receive it.*

"This promised blessing, if claimed by faith,
would bring all other blessings in its train, and it is to
be given liberally to the people of God. Through the
cunning devices of the enemy the minds of God's
people seem to be incapable of comprehending and
appropriating the promises of God. They seem to
think that only the scantiest showers of grace are to
fall upon the thirsty soul. The people of God have
accustomed themselves to think that they must rely
upon their own efforts, that little help is to be received from heaven; and the result is that they have
little light to communicate to other souls who are
dying in error and darkness. The church has long
been contented with little of the blessing of God;
they have not felt the need of reaching up to the exalted privileges purchased for them at infinite cost.
Their spiritual strength has been feeble, their experience of a dwarfed and crippled character, and they
are disqualified for the work the Lord would have
them to do. They are not able to present the great
and glorious truths of God's holy word that would
convict and convert souls through the agency of the
Holy Spirit. The power of God awaits their demand
and reception. A harvest of joy will be reaped by
those who sow the holy seeds of truth."—*Testimonies
to Ministers,* pp. 174, 175. (Italics mine.)

*       *       *

And now a prefatory word on the significance of the last four chapters, on the symbols of the Spirit.

The matchless provision of the Holy Spirit's ministry, to meet man's need, is the last link in the chain of divine love with which our God in heaven has bound Himself to man on earth. Not only was the Spirit the instrument in the original creation of the world and of mankind, but it was through the Eternal Spirit that our precious Redeemer became incarnate in human flesh, and offered Himself for man's complete reconciliation and his full salvation. And it is by means of the selfsame Spirit of God that the miracle of regeneration of human hearts has been accomplished through the ages, and also that the indwelling Christ is made blessedly possible in these body temples of ours. So it is obvious that the Holy Spirit is the divinely appointed connecting link between heaven and earth.

Well may we pause and ponder this profound truth and provision. The majesty of His person, the power of His might, and the scope of His work will never be fully understood or adequately set forth. But as the light of the Word is focused anew in reverent contemplation upon fresh angles of His operations, we catch added gleams of God's glorious provision, and our hearts thrill in responsive adoration. Praise be to our Father for His boundless love and limitless provision for our every need.

The theme of the office and work of the Holy

Spirit offers a field for exhaustless study, because it deals with a timeless and measureless Personality—the third person of the Godhead. His stately steppings cannot be measured, but they may be clearly recognized; they cannot be explained, but they can and must be personally accepted and experienced. Richer than all the fabled jewels of earth are these symbolic gems from heaven's storehouse—presented under the figures of wind, water, fire, and oil—which, as we gaze into their depths of meaning, disclose a charm and beauty scarcely discernible under unfigurative phraseology.

May the matchless Spirit of truth, to whom these tributes are inscribed, guide our thought in study, illuminate our minds in meditation, and possess our souls for action so completely and exclusively that His holy work, portrayed under these illuminating figures chosen by Him, shall be entirely wrought out in the life. So, blessed Spirit, meet Thou our souls' deep need; satisfy the longing of our hearts; fit us for sacred service, and then use us to the glory of the Father and the Son for the finishing of our committed task. Yea, possess us as Thy very own, both now and forevermore.                                            L. E. F.

# Part I

## The Promise of the Spirit

# My King Divine

1. JESUS, Thou radiant King,
   Monarch divine;
   Reign Thou within this heart
   Thy love has won.
   Take Thou this yielded throne,
   Thy will be done;
   Live Thou Thy life within,
   My King divine.

CHORUS: My King divine, my King divine,
   Live Thou Thy life within, my King divine.

2. Keep through temptation's hour,
   Saviour divine;
   Meet Thou the wily foe,
   Thy power display.
   Give vict'ry hour by hour,
   O'er all the way;
   Lead on triumphantly,
   My King divine.

3. Use me in time's last hour,
   Master divine;
   Fit me for service, Lord,
   Thy love to tell.
   Win souls Thyself through me,
   Thy praise to swell;
   Grant Thou my heart's desire,
   My King divine.

[It was during the time of preparatory study for these presentations, when the heart was full of love and wonder over new glimpses of God's matchless provision of the Holy Spirit for our need, and the complete claim of His love upon us was seen as never before, that this hymn was born—the music at the noon hour and the words in the evening of the same day. So it rightfully belongs with these studies on the Holy Spirit.—L. E. F.]

‹‹‹-‹‹‹-‹‹‹-‹‹‹-‹‹‹

# The Promise of the Spirit

"LITTLE children, yet a little while I am with you. Ye shall seek Me: and as I said unto the Jews, Whither I go, ye cannot come; so now I say to you. . . . Simon Peter said unto Him, Lord, whither goest Thou? Jesus answered him, Whither I go, thou canst not follow Me now; but thou shalt follow Me afterwards." John 13:33-36.

"Let not your heart be troubled: ye believe in God, believe also in Me. In My Father's house are many mansions: if it were not so, I would have told you. I go to prepare a place for you. And if I go and prepare a place for you, I will come again, and receive you unto Myself; that where I am, there ye may be also. And whither I go ye know, and the way ye know." John 14:1-4.

"Philip saith unto Him, Lord, shew us the Father, and it sufficeth us. Jesus saith unto him, Have I been so long time with you, and yet hast thou not known Me, Philip? he that hath seen Me hath seen the Father; and how sayest thou then, Shew us the Father? Believest thou not that I am in the Father, and the Father in Me? the words that I speak unto you I speak not of Myself: but the Father that dwell-

eth in Me, He doeth the works. Believe Me that I am
in the Father, and the Father in Me: or else believe
Me for the very works' sake. Verily, verily, I say
unto you, He that believeth on Me, the works that I
do shall he do also; and greater works than these
shall he do; because I go unto My Father." Verses
8-12.

"I will pray the Father, and He shall give you another Comforter, that He may abide with you for
ever; even the Spirit of truth; whom the world cannot receive, because it seeth Him not, neither knoweth Him: but ye know Him; for He dwelleth with
you, and shall be in you. I will not leave you comfortless: I will come to you. Yet a little while, and
the world seeth Me no more; but ye see Me: because
I live, ye shall live also. At that day ye shall know
that I am in My Father, and ye in Me, and I in you."
Verses 16-20.

"Jesus answered and said unto him, If a man
love Me, he will keep My words: and My Father will
love him, and we will come unto him, and make our
abode with him. He that loveth Me not keepeth not
My sayings: and the word which ye hear is not Mine,
but the Father's which sent Me. These things have I
spoken unto you, being yet present with you." Verses
23-25.

"Nevertheless I tell you the truth; It is expedient
for you that I go away: for if I go not away, the Comforter will not come unto you; but if I depart, I will

send Him unto you. And when He is come, He will reprove the world of sin, and of righteousness, and of judgment: of sin, because they believe not on Me; of righteousness, because I go to My Father, and ye see Me no more; of judgment, because the prince of this world is judged. I have yet many things to say unto you, but ye cannot bear them now. Howbeit when He, the Spirit of truth, is come, He will guide you into all truth: for He shall not speak of Himself; but whatsoever He shall hear, that shall He speak: and He will shew you things to come. He shall glorify Me: for He shall receive of Mine, and shall shew it unto you. All things that the Father hath are Mine: therefore said I, that He shall take of Mine, and shall shew it unto you." John 16:7-15.

≪≪-≪≪-≪≪-≪≪-≪≪-

# The Promise of the Spirit

IT was night in Jerusalem—the saddest night since man separated himself from God. The city was thronged with worshipers. The little group of men who had followed their Lord through the years of His public ministry had gathered with Him about the paschal table in the upper room. It was an epochal hour. Type was touching antitype. The Son of God, girding Himself with a towel as a servant, had knelt before sinful men and washed their feet.

They had eaten the broken bread and had drunk the poured-out wine—the symbols of His approaching passion. Only a few minutes separated the scenes of the upper room from the struggle in the garden; just a few moments, comparatively, between the blood on the brow and the blood on the doorpost. For a little while the Shepherd had been with the sheep, but soon the Shepherd would be smitten and the sheep scattered.

Judas had left the group, and the other disciples were filled with sadness. It is not necessary to analyze their sorrow. There was much of selfishness intermingled with it. But the shadow of the approaching separation had fallen upon them. It was indeed a momentous hour. How they listen to Jesus' every word! His declaration that He was going where they could not follow brought sorrow and grief to their hearts. They had not before sensed the reality of the coming separation.

The Master proceeds to apply comfort to their hearts. He tells of mansions He is going to prepare for them. But that does not compensate. Mansions cannot take the place of the personal presence of their living Lord. What would they do when He was gone? To whom could they turn?

As someone has said, Paint a starless sky. Drape the mountains with darkness. Hang somber curtains of black on every shore. Darken the past, and let the future be even more bleak. Fill the picture with sad-faced, sorrow-shrouded men. Such was the disciples' situation, as they faced their Lord's departure.

### Jesus Introduces His Successor

Then He proceeded to unfold to them the wondrous provision of "another Comforter." This statement implies that Jesus was the *first* Comforter. A comforter is a "help in time of need." If one is an orphan, he needs a parent; if sick, he needs a doctor; if perplexed, a lawyer; if he is going to build, an architect; if in trouble, a friend.

All this and infinitely more is our heavenly Comforter. The disciples were not to be left orphans, bereft of a divine parent to care for, protect, and help them. At the most impressionable moment of their lives He taught them of the coming of the Holy Spirit as the culmination and continuation of His work on earth for them.

To receive the Holy Spirit was their supreme privilege, and is likewise to be the supreme privilege of every disciple of that same Lord, while waiting for His visible, bodily return to receive them to the heavenly mansions. Note this:

"In the teachings of Christ, the doctrine of the Holy Spirit is made prominent. What a vast theme is this for contemplation and encouragement! What treasures of truth did He add to the knowledge of His disciples in His instruction concerning the Holy Spirit, the Comforter! He dwelt upon this theme in order to console His disciples in the great trial they were soon to experience, that they might be cheered in their great disappointment. . . . The world's Redeemer sought to bring to the hearts of the sorrowing disciples the strongest solace. But from a large field of subjects, He chose the theme of the Holy Spirit, which was to inspire and comfort their hearts. And yet, though Christ made much of this theme concerning the Holy Spirit, how little is it dwelt upon in the churches!"—MRS. E. G. WHITE in *Bible Echo,* Nov. 15, 1893.

Before vacating His own earthly office as teacher, Jesus introduced His successor in His valedictory discourse.

"Cumbered with humanity, Christ could not be in

every place personally. Therefore it was for their interest that He should go to the Father, and send the Spirit to be His successor on earth."—*The Desire of Ages,* p. 669.

He unfolded the tremendous fact of the dispensation of the Spirit, and this dispensational aspect cannot be overemphasized. It is based on the earthly work of Christ, and its coming was impossible until that work was finished and He ascended. In John 14 and 16 Jesus opened before them the three mighty truths of—(1) the promised coming of the Holy Spirit; (2) the character and personality of the Holy Spirit; and (3) the mission, or work, of the Holy Spirit.

### The Dispensation of the Spirit

Taking these in order, observe first the explicit declaration of the coming of the Holy Spirit. One must be impressed with the fact that just as truly as the prophets announced Jesus' advent, so He announces the advent of another, coequal with Himself and the successor of Himself. As one ascended, so the other descended. And the same recognition of authority and deference paid by the disciples to their Lord, was to be given to the Holy Spirit as Christ's vicar on earth.

As Christ had a definite time mission, so the Holy Spirit likewise has a definite time mission, His special dispensation being from Pentecost to the Second Advent. He is a person of the Godhead who came to earth in a definite way, at a definite time, for a definite work, and has been here ever since, just as really as Jesus was here on His special mission during the thirty-three years.

"The dispensation in which we are now living is to be, to those that ask, the dispensation of the Holy Spirit."—*Testimonies to Ministers,* p. 511.

We are under the direct, personal guidance of the third person of the Godhead as truly as the disciples were under the leadership of the second person.

Pentecost was, as it were, the inaugural of the Holy Spirit for this special work, though the Holy Spirit was existent and operative from the ages past. Many a biography of Christ begins with Bethlehem and ends with Olivet, despite the fact that He was from the days of eternity.

Eighty-eight times, and in twenty-two of the thirty-nine books of the Old Testament, the Spirit is mentioned. The footprints of the third person of the Godhead may be traced through the centuries from the beginning of the world.

### Old Testament Relationships

At creation the Holy Spirit was present, brooding over chaos, and was the agency in producing cosmos. He is also spoken of in definite connection with men. But before Pentecost He came more as a transient visitor, for the purpose of equipping certain men for their special work. His action was more intermittent than constant. He came upon individuals, working through or clothing them with mighty power for special deeds. He strove with men (Gen. 6:3); He gave Bezaleel skill (Ex. 31:3-5); He gave Samson strength (Judges 14:6). Thus did the Holy Spirit make men His instruments, doing a work or delivering messages through them, as with Joshua (Num. 27:18), Gideon (Judges 6:34), Saul (1 Sam. 10:10), and David (1 Sam. 16:13). We read:

"During the patriarchal age, the influence of the Holy Spirit had often been revealed in a marked manner, but never in its fulness. Now, in obedience to the word of the Saviour, the disciples offered their supplications for this gift, and in heaven Christ added His intercession. He claimed the gift of the Spirit, that He might pour it upon His people."—*Acts of the Apostles,* p. 37.

It is a significant fact that in the Old Testament the Spirit is never spoken of as the Comforter, or the "Spirit of Jesus" (Phil. 1:19), or the "Spirit of His [God's] Son" (Gal. 4:6), and similar expressions, but as of God the Father. Why are all these new titles found in the New Testament? Ah! something has happened! An event has occurred that has changed things!

Jesus was born and died for us, arose from the grave and ascended. And when Jesus completed His work on earth and ascended with His glorified humanity, taking His place in the heavenlies, then the conditions were fulfilled, and the Holy Spirit came down as Christ's official representative and successor to make individually efficacious that redemptive work. So He comes transcendently as the Spirit of Jesus.

## The New Testament Provision

It may be of interest, in passing, to note that the Holy Spirit is mentioned two hundred and sixty-two times in the New Testament—a veritable battalion of texts. Behind it all is the finished work and the glorified person of our adorable Lord. Reasoning back from a glorified Jesus, we see it was because of His obedience unto death to bring us to God, through the vicarious substitution of His own sinless life and atoning death, meeting the demands of righteousness and justice as well as of holiness. Thus the Holy Spirit came in recognition of the Father's acceptance, and for the assurance of man. "By one offering He hath perfected for ever them that are sanctified. Whereof the Holy Ghost also is a witness to us." Heb. 10:14, 15.

Consider the twofold work of the Holy Spirit. In the Old Testament He worked upon men more from without inward, but did not dwell or abide in them permanently. He appeared to them and empowered them, but did not often take up His abode in them. But from Pentecost onward there has been a great change. His is now a special work, differing from that of preceding ages. Provision is made for Him to enter and live in all Christian believers, and to work from within outward, filling and abiding.

This personal indwelling of the Divine Spirit is the distinctive glory of the Christian dispensation. Everything in the past was preparatory to this. The Old Testament provision was the promise and preparation: the New, the fulfillment and possession. The difference is between simply *inworking* and *indwelling*. And it is a permanent heritage; He is to abide thus with us forever.

### Gift of Father Through the Son

The coming of the Holy Spirit was as the *gift* of the Father through the Son. (John 14:16.) Christ's praying, or asking, the Father indicates in the Greek word a petition from one on a perfect equality. Yet He did not ask for the Holy Spirit in the marvelous prayer which immediately follows in chapter 17. Why? Because His passion was not yet accomplished.

When the Spirit came it was in vindication of the character of the ministry and the completed sacrificial mission of the Son. (John 14:23-26.) It was based upon the finished work of Calvary. It was the glorified Christ who asked for, received, and sent the Holy Spirit upon the waiting disciples.

The Holy Spirit is Himself the gift of God to man. He cannot be bought, earned, discovered, or evolved. Man had no claim upon God for such a gift. The Holy Spirit was not poured out in answer to any mere prayer of man, or in response to any merit of man. But because of the work Jesus wrought, and the satisfaction given, the righteous God sent the Holy Spirit for the initiation of a new movement among men, and to usher in the new dispensation.

The gift of the Spirit Himself must be distinguished from the gifts the Holy Spirit bestows. As the Roman emperors, making a triumphal entry into Rome, cast the coin of the conquered kingdoms to the multitudes, so Christ, after His triumphal procession into heaven, gave this Gift supreme to men. Of course, the most conspicuous culmination of all the gifts the Holy Spirit bestows upon the remnant church has been the restoration of the gift of the Spirit of prophecy. But that is a different matter.

### Relationship of Calvary and Pentecost

The baptism of the Holy Spirit is declared by John the Baptist to be the essential, vital purpose of the ministry of Jesus Christ. "I indeed baptize you with water unto repentance: but He that cometh after me is mightier than I, whose shoes I am not worthy to bear: He shall baptize you with the Holy Ghost, and with fire." Matt. 3:11. (See also John 1:33.)

John's message concerning Christ was twofold —the blood of the Lamb taking away sin, and the baptism of the Spirit to keep from sin, or Calvary and Pentecost. The culmination of Calvary for this dispensation is found in the gift of the Holy Spirit by Jesus Christ. They are two inseparable truths. Without Calvary there could be no Pentecost; and without Pentecost, Calvary is of little avail. Just observe this:

"The Holy Spirit was the highest of all gifts that He could solicit from His Father for the exaltation of His people. The Spirit was to be given as a regenerating agent, and without this the sacrifice of Christ would have been of no avail. The power of evil had been strengthening for centuries, and the submission of men to this satanic captivity was amazing. Sin could be resisted and overcome only through the mighty agency of the third person of the Godhead, who would come with no modified energy, but in the fulness of divine power. It is the Spirit that makes effectual what has been wrought out by the world's Redeemer. It is by the Spirit that the heart is made pure. Through the Spirit the believer becomes a partaker of the divine nature. Christ has given His Spirit as a divine power to overcome all hereditary and cultivated tendencies to evil, and to impress His own character upon His church."—*The Desire of Ages,* p. 671.

If it were not for the atmosphere that surrounds our earth, the sun, though a ball of fire, would shine upon us coldly like a twinkling star. The atmosphere enveloping the earth receives its rays and transmutes them into color, heat, and light. Likewise, were it not for the Holy Spirit, Christ seated at the right hand of the Father could be worshiped only as a risen, ascended Lord. But the Holy Spirit reveals Him to our hearts as the light, the life, and the truth.

And as when we look through the telescope, we see not the lens but the object the lens brings near, so through the Holy Spirit we see not Him, but "Jesus only." The cross is much more easily comprehended, for the pouring out of the blood is visible and outward, and is for all; whereas this gift of the Spirit is inward and invisible, and is for the loving, obedient disciple. His indwelling, being spiritual, is not so readily grasped and made a practical reality.

The blood of Calvary cleanses the soul temple. Yet there is more in God's provision. Then nothing less than occupancy through the indwelling Spirit will satisfy either God or man.

### Christ's Personal Presence Localized

The baptism of the Spirit was not accomplished during the three years of Christ's earthly ministry. It was impossible because of the localization and limitations of His humanity, and for the reason that "the Holy Ghost was not yet given; because that Jesus was not yet glorified." John 7:39. So Jesus never baptized with the Holy Spirit during His earthly career.

Among His last words was the charge to wait for the promised baptism after His departure. "And, being assembled together with them, commanded them that they should not depart from Jerusalem, but wait for the promise of the Father, which, saith He, ye have heard of Me. For John truly baptized with water; but ye shall be baptized with the Holy Ghost not many days hence." Acts 1:4, 5.

He who was to baptize His followers with the Holy Spirit was the example of all He desires to put into our lives. He was begotten of the Spirit. He grew up under the power and tutelage of the Spirit. At the threshold of His ministry He was specially anointed for service by the Spirit. He lived His life, performed His miracles, and taught His principles in the power of the Spirit. And He arose from the dead by the power of the Spirit. From the cradle to the grave He was indwelt by the Holy Ghost.

"Christ's humanity was united with divinity; He was fitted for the conflict by the indwelling of the Holy Spirit. And He came to make us partakers of the divine nature."—*Ibid.,* p. 123.

Be it remembered that Christ's incarnation, sinless life, and atoning death, His resurrection, ascension, and entrance upon His heavenly mediatorial work were absolutely indispensable, and at the same time were preliminary steps toward this one thing: "Christ hath redeemed us from the curse of the law, being made a curse for us: for it is written, Cursed is every one that hangeth on a tree: that the blessing of Abraham might come on the Gentiles through Jesus Christ; that we might receive the promise of the Spirit through faith." Gal. 3:13, 14.

## Goal of Present Redemption

And this goal of present redemption was impossible before His glorification. (John 7:39.) Thus Peter says, "Therefore being by the right hand of God exalted, and having received of the Father the promise of the Holy Ghost, He hath shed forth this, which ye now see and hear." Acts 2:33.

The rock in Horeb was a type. The smiting of the rock brought the flowing water. So the outpouring of the Holy Spirit was in answer to Christ's atoning death. His death removed every barrier between God and the sinner. (2 Cor. 5:19.) The Father's acceptance of the Son's sacrifice was the indispensable condition to our justification.

But only the coming of the Holy Spirit could apply the results of that sacrifice, making effectual in us what Jesus did for us. Having perfected His human nature, Jesus could now communicate what was previously impossible. And the Holy Spirit's work in this dispensation is that of applying and communicating the atoning work of Christ to individual human hearts, regenerating, justifying, sanctifying, and communicating the very life of our risen Lord, as we await His second bodily coming.

# CHAPTER TWO

# The Personality of the Spirit

Now think of the Holy Spirit's *character*. He is "another Comforter." This identifies the promised Spirit with the promising Lord in being, character, purpose, and activity. He is Christ's other self, as it were, identical in nature and character. If a crude simile may be permitted, they are like two sides of a triangle—alike and related, but different. Note this:

"The Holy Spirit was not yet fully manifested; for Christ had not yet been glorified. The more abundant impartation of the Spirit did not take place till after Christ's ascension. Not until this was received could the disciples fulfil the commission to preach the gospel to the world. But the Spirit was now given for a special purpose. Before the disciples could fulfil their official duties in connection with the church, Christ breathed His Spirit upon them. He was committing to them a most sacred trust, and He desired to impress them with the fact that without the Holy Spirit this work could not be accomplished.

"The Holy Spirit is the breath of spiritual life in the soul. The impartation of the Spirit is the impartation of the life of Christ. It imbues the receiver with the attributes of Christ."—*The Desire of Ages,* p. 805.

Jesus said of Himself: "The Spirit of the Lord is upon Me, because He hath anointed Me to preach the gospel to the poor; He hath sent Me to heal the brokenhearted, to preach deliverance to the captives, and recovering of sight to the blind, to set at liberty them that are bruised, to preach the acceptable year of the Lord." Luke 4:18, 19. You cannot heal the brokenhearted without the Comforter—one alongside to help. They were to lose Him, the first Comforter, so He would send another. As long as Christ lives, so long does that pledge stand.

## The Ministry of the Paraclete

But *Comforter* is an inadequate translation of the Greek word *Parakletos,* the new name for the new ministry upon which the Spirit was about to enter. *Paraclete* is better translated *advocate,* most scholars say. It also means representative, intercessor, pleader, consoler. Really it is an untranslatable term. It is the same word used of Christ with reference to His work before the Father: "My little children, these things write I unto you, that ye sin not. And if any man sin, we have an advocate with the Father, Jesus Christ the righteous." 1 John 2:1.

In Greece and Rome, during New Testament times, the advocate helped the client in two different ways: Sometimes he spoke for him before the tribunal, pleading his case for him; at other times he merely prepared his speech for him, that the client might speak for himself. So Christ is our advocate with the Father, and the Holy Spirit is Christ's advocate with us.

As Christ pleads for us, so the Spirit pleads for Christ in our hearts. Shall we who do all honor to the representatives of earthly governments, be guilty of disrespect and neglect of this Advocate of the heavenly King, Christ's representative to the church and to the world?

### The Spirit a Divine Person

The discussion of the character of the Holy Spirit leads us directly into a consideration of His *personality*. It is easy to think of the Father as a person, and Jesus as a person. We seem to "visualize" them, as it were. But the Holy Spirit is considered so mysterious, and is so invisible, so secret, and His acts are so removed from the senses, that His personality is questioned because contrasted with the other persons of the Godhead.

He has, of course, appeared visibly to the human senses, taking for occasion the form of a dove. (Luke 3:22.) Then, too, much is said of His influence, graces, power, and gifts. So we are prone to think of Him only as an influence, a power, an energy. Such symbols as wind, fire, oil, water, and so forth, have tended in that direction.

Moreover, the fact that the name *Spirit* in the Greek, is neuter, and in following precise grammatical construction the impersonal pronoun *itself* is used in the Authorized Version in Romans 8:16, 26, has had a large bearing on the popular understanding —"The Spirit itself beareth witness with our spirit, that we are the children of God"; "likewise the Spirit also helpeth our infirmities: for we know not what we should pray for as we ought: but the Spirit itself maketh intercession for us with groanings which cannot be uttered." These have been corrected, however, in the Revised Version to harmonize with His personality.

### A Question of Utmost Importance

This is not a mere technical, academic, or impractical question. It is of utmost importance and highest practical value. If He is a divine person, and we think of Him as an impersonal influence, we are robbing a divine person of the deference, honor, and love that is His due. Again, if the Holy Spirit is a mere influence or power, we shall try to get hold of and use *it*. But if we recognize Him as a person, we shall study how to yield to Him, that He may use us.

If we think we have the Holy Spirit, we shall be inclined to strutting and self-inflation; but the other, the true concept, leads to self-renunciation, self-abnegation, and self-humiliation. Nothing is more calculated to lay the glory of man in the dust. On this point let us again note the Spirit of prophecy:

"We cannot use the Holy Spirit; the Spirit is to use us. Through the Spirit, God works in His people 'to will and to do of His good pleasure.' But many will not submit to be led. They want to manage themselves. This is why they do not receive the heavenly gift. Only to those who wait humbly upon God, who watch for His guidance and grace, is the Spirit given. This promised blessing, claimed by faith, brings all other blessings in its train. It is given according to the riches of the grace of Christ, and He is ready to supply every soul according to the capacity to receive."—*Gospel Workers,* p. 285.

No, the Holy Spirit is not a thin, shadowy effluence emanating from the Father. He is not an impersonal something to be vaguely recognized, just an invisible principle of life. The Holy Spirit has in the minds of multitudes been separated from personality, made intangible, unreal, hidden in mists and shrouded with unreality. But the greatest unseen reality in the world today is the Holy Spirit. He is a holy personality.

Jesus was the most marked and influential personality ever in this old world, and the Holy Spirit was to supply His vacated place. No one but a person could take the place of that wondrous Person. No mere influence would ever suffice.

### The Nature of Personality

There is danger of limiting our idea of personality to bodily manifestations. It seems difficult to grasp the idea of personality apart from the tangible bodily form of humanity—existence with a limited, human, bodily shape. But personality and such corporeality are to be clearly distinguished, though they are often confused. Personality does not require the limitations of humanity. Here again the Spirit of prophecy speaks:

"The Holy Spirit is Christ's representative, but divested of the personality of humanity, and independent thereof. Cumbered with humanity, Christ could not be in every place personally. Therefore it was for their interest that He should go to the Father, and send the Spirit to be His successor on earth. No one could then have any advantage because of his location or his personal contact with Christ. By the Spirit the Saviour would be accessible to all. In this sense He would be nearer to them than if He had not ascended on high."—*The Desire of Ages,* p. 669.

God the Spirit is not to be measured by human standards. We cannot express the infinite in finite terms. The Holy Spirit is incapable of concise, final definition. We need not solve the mystery of His nature. Against this we are specifically warned:

"It is not essential for us to be able to define just what the Holy Spirit is. Christ tells us that the Spirit is the Comforter, 'the Spirit of truth, which proceedeth from the Father.' It is plainly declared regarding the Holy Spirit, that in His work of guiding men into all truth, 'He shall not speak of Himself.'

"The nature of the Holy Spirit is a mystery. Men

cannot explain it, because the Lord has not revealed it to them. Men having fanciful views may bring together passages of Scripture and put a human construction on them; but the acceptance of these views will not strengthen the church. Regarding such mysteries, which are too deep for human understanding, silence is golden."—*Acts of the Apostles,* pp. 51, 52.

Here is further important counsel:

"There are those who, in their present state, would interpose between God and those who need the light. They would not understand the work of the Holy Spirit; they have never understood it; in the past it has been to them as great a mystery as were Christ's lessons to the Jews. The working of the Holy Spirit of God is not to create curiosity. It is not for men to decide whether they shall lay their hands upon the manifestations of the Spirit of God. We must let God work."—*Counsels to Teachers,* p. 373.

### Third Person of the Godhead

But the same inspired instruction establishes forever the fact of His personality. He is the "Third *Person* of the Godhead":

"Evil had been accumulating for centuries, and could only be restrained and resisted by the mighty power of the Holy Spirit, the third person of the Godhead, who would come with no modified energy, but in the fullness of divine power."—*Testimonies to Ministers,* p. 392.

There are "three living Persons" in the heavenly trio:

"The Father is all the fulness of the Godhead bodily, and is invisible to mortal sight.

"The Son [of God] is all the fulness of the Godhead manifested. The Word of God declares Him to be 'the express image of His person.' 'God so loved the world, that He gave His only begotten Son, that whosoever believeth in Him should not perish, but have everlasting life.' Here is shown the personality of the Father.

"The Comforter that Christ promised to send after He ascended to heaven, is the Spirit in all the fulness of the Godhead, making manifest the power of divine grace to all who receive and believe in Christ as a personal Saviour. There are three living persons of the heavenly trio; in the name of these three great powers—the Father, the Son, and the Holy Spirit—those who receive Christ by living faith are baptized, and these powers will co-operate with the obedient subjects of heaven in their efforts to live the new life in Christ."—*Testimonies,* Series B, no. 7, pp. 62, 63.

### Four Predications of Personality

God is not a magnified or sublimated man. God alone has perfect personality. His perfect personality has existed since the days of eternity, long before a single human being, with his limitations, came to be. There are four things that are predicated of personality: (1) will, (2) intelligence, (3) power, (4) capacity for love. Personality therefore involves a self-conscious, self-knowing, self-willing, and self-determining being.

A person is a being who is approachable, who can be trusted or doubted, loved or hated, adored or insulted. These essentials of personality are but limited and imperfect in man, but limitless and perfect in God. So the personality of the Holy Spirit is not to be confined to comparisons with man.

It will help us to listen to Jesus on this point in these two chapters of John, the fourteenth and sixteenth. Not a word does Jesus utter that can be construed as implying that the Holy Spirit is simply an influence. He addresses Him and treats Him as a person. He calls Him the Paraclete, which is a title that could be held only by a person.

The idea of personality dominates the grammatical construction of His sentences. Twenty-four times in John 14, 15, and 16 the personal pronouns *He, Him,* and *whom* occur, applied to the Spirit. (For example, note John 15:26 and 16:13.) Not that the persons of the Godhead are masculine as contrasted with feminine, but personal as contrasted with impersonal.

In certain texts the personality of the Spirit is held subordinate to emphasize some other characteristic. If the personality is understood, the pronoun *it* is wholly proper. The Spirit is set forth by Christ as teaching, speaking, bearing witness, guiding, hearing, and declaring. Here are intelligence, discrimination, and therefore personality.

### Personal Relations Are Ascribed

Now let us take a rapid survey of the Bible testimony as to the personality of the Holy Spirit. Personal qualities, personal actions, and personal relations are ascribed to Him. It is knowledge, feeling, will, and love, not hands or feet, that are the marks of personality.

1. KNOWLEDGE.—"What man knoweth the things of a man, save the spirit of man which is in him? even so the things of God knoweth no man, but the Spirit of God." 1 Cor. 2:11. The Holy Spirit is a person qualified to deal with personal beings consciously and intelligently, causing them to know what is in the heart of God for them, and what is in their own hearts. It is preposterous to speak of an influence, energy, or power as having such understanding.

2. WILL.—"All these worketh that one and the selfsame Spirit, dividing to every man severally as He will." 1 Cor. 12:11. Here is the strongest proof of personality. The will is the most distinctive element in any personality.

3. MIND.—"He that searcheth the hearts knoweth what is the mind of the Spirit, because He maketh

intercession for the saints according to the will of God." Rom. 8:27. This in the Greek implies both thought and purpose. An exhibition of this is found in Acts 15:28: "It seemed good to the Holy Ghost, and to us, to lay upon you no greater burden than these necessary things." Thus we read:

"Through the power of the Holy Spirit, every work of God's appointment is to be elevated and ennobled, and made to witness for the Lord. Man must place himself under the control of the eternal mind, whose dictates he is to obey in every particular."—*Counsels on Health,* p. 524.

4. LOVE.—"Now I beseech you, brethren, for the Lord Jesus Christ's sake, and for the love of the Spirit." Rom. 15:30. The Holy Spirit is not blind power but a person who loves with tenderest affection.

5. COMMUNION.—"The grace of the Lord Jesus Christ, and the love of God, and the communion of the Holy Ghost, be with you all." 2 Cor. 13:14. He is thus bound up with the supreme personalities, the Father and the Son, in the apostolic benediction. And communion with the Holy Spirit is conceivable only on the basis of personality. It implies partnership and reciprocity.

6. GRIEF.—"Grieve not the holy Spirit of God, whereby ye are sealed unto the day of redemption." Eph. 4:30. How the realization of this thought as related to this holy person will shape the whole life!

7. INSULTED, TEMPTED, AND LIED TO.—Note these scriptures: "Of how much sorer punishment, suppose ye, shall he be thought worthy, who hath trodden under foot the Son of God, and hath counted the blood of the covenant, wherewith he was sanctified, an unholy thing, and hath done despite unto the Spirit of grace?" Heb. 10:29. "Then Peter said unto her, How is it that ye have agreed together to tempt the Spirit of the Lord? behold, the feet of them which have buried thy husband are at the door, and shall carry thee out." Acts 5:9 "Peter said, Ananias, why hath Satan filled thine heart to lie to the Holy Ghost? . . . Thou hast not lied unto me, but unto God." Acts 5:3, 4. Thus He is susceptible to personal mistreatment.

### Divine Attributes and Works

In the four Gospels the most solemn warning ever uttered by Jesus in the hearing of men declared that if His own words or person were rejected, the rejecter could be forgiven, but he could not be forgiven if he grieved and sinned against the Holy Spirit and finally refused His teachings. It is inconceivable that man should so sin against an influence, power, or energy as to bring himself into danger of unpardonable sin.

Let us next sweep through the acts and deeds ascribed to Him, that only a person could perform. Think of His inspiring of the Sacred Writings, His commands and forbiddings, His appointments of ministers, His intercessions and prayers, His teaching and witnessing, His convicting and striving. There are some twenty different actions declared, the greatest acts possible for intelligent personality, which could not be performed by an influence.

But the Holy Spirit is more than a mere personality. He is a divine person. He is called God (Acts 5:3, 4), the "third person of the Godhead." He possesses *divine attributes:* omnipotence (Luke 1:35), omnipresence (Ps. 139:7-10), and eternal life (Heb. 9:14). These pertain only to God, yet they are attributes of the Spirit. He is greater than the angels, for He, as the representative of Christ, directs all the angels on earth in battle with the legions of darkness.

"All the intelligences of heaven are in this army. And more than angels are in the ranks. The Holy Spirit, the representative of the Captain of the Lord's host, comes down to direct the battle."—*The Desire of Ages,* p. 352.

Again, *divine works* are predicated of Him: creation (Job 33:4), regeneration (John 3:5-8), resurrection (1 Peter 3:18), and authorship of prophecy (2 Peter 1:21). These works could be accomplished by God alone. Therefore the Holy Spirit is not only a person but a divine person. In the divine plan His ministry includes creation, inspiration, conviction, regeneration, sanctification, and equipment for effective service.

## Relationship to the Godhead

This brings us to a brief survey of the relationship of the Holy Spirit to the other persons of the Godhead. In our conception of the Trinity we are sometimes inclined to conceive of three Gods instead of one. Our God is one God (Deut. 6:4); but there are three persons in the one Godhead. Our difficulty arises from trying to conceive of spiritual beings in terms of the physical. Perhaps a crude illustration may be suggestive. A triangle is one figure, but it has three sides. So the Godhead, being one, is manifested as Father, Son, and Holy Spirit. Jesus said, "I and My Father are one." John 10:30.

Here is a helpful statement:

" 'If ye had known Me,' Christ said, 'ye should have known My Father also; and from henceforth ye know Him, and have seen Him.' But not yet did the disciples understand. 'Lord, show us the Father,' exclaimed Philip, 'and it sufficeth us.'

"Amazed at his dullness of comprehension, Christ asked with pained surprise, 'Have I been so long time with you, and yet hast thou not known Me, Philip?' Is it possible that you do not see the Father in the works He does through Me? Do you not believe that I came to testify of the Father? 'How sayest thou then, Show us the Father?' 'He that hath seen Me hath seen the Father.' Christ had not ceased to be God when He became man. Though He had humbled

Himself to humanity, the Godhead was still His own."—*Ibid.,* pp. 663, 664.

Again, in speaking of the coming of the Holy Spirit, Christ said:

"I will pray the Father, and He shall give you another Comforter, . . . the Spirit of truth. . . . *I* will not leave you comfortless: *I* will come to you." John 14:16-18. "My Father will love him, and we will come unto him, and make our abode with him." Verse 23.

So the presence of the Holy Spirit involves the presence of Jesus and the Father. In other words, the fullness of the Godhead is operative and present in the world in this dispensation by the Holy Spirit. Thus the Holy Spirit is, as it were, Jesus' other self. And Jesus thus makes His universal and abiding presence in all His people.

"Those who see Christ in His true character, and receive Him into the heart, have everlasting life. It is through the Spirit that Christ dwells in us; and the Spirit of God, received into the heart by faith, is the beginning of the life eternal."—*Ibid.,* p. 388.

### Three Consecutive Dispensations

Before Christ came in the flesh, the Father was the most conspicuous person of the Godhead, filling the horizon; when Jesus came, the second person filled the horizon; and in this dispensation of the Spirit, the third person fills the horizon, this latter being the culmination of God's progressive provisions.

In the dispensation of the Father the standard of the law was outstanding; in the dispensation of the Son, reconciliation is added; and in the dispensation of the Spirit, sanctifying, equipping power. Thus they are cumulative. Each reinforces and supplements the other.

In each dispensation the spirituality of the church has been conditioned upon adherence to the principal truth of the economy in which it lives. The standard of righteousness has been set forth, the means of reconciliation and atonement made manifest, and lastly the agent for applying this benefit to man now conspicuously occupies the field.

The three great historic tests of faith as regards godliness are: *first,* in the period before the incarnation, the test of "one God" versus polytheism, and God's right to rule, with the law as the standard and the Sabbath as the sign; *second,* as to whether, at Christ's first advent, those who had met the first test would accept Jesus as the divine Son and Redeemer; then, *third,* having accepted the first two, as to whether we will submit fully to the Holy Spirit to make efficacious *in* us all that has been wrought out *for* us.

These are broad fundamentals, and sweep everything vital to the divine plan of salvation into their embrace.

## The Godhead a Trinity

The plurality of the Godhead is first indicated in Genesis 1:26, when God said, "Let us make man in our image." The Father is the source, the Son the intermediary, and the Holy Spirit is the medium through which the creation came into being.

The trinity of the Godhead is several times implied in the Old Testament. In Numbers 6:24-27, "They shall put My *name* upon the children of Israel," and it proceeds with the expansion, "The Lord . . . the Lord . . . the Lord"—not four times, or two, but three: "The Lord bless thee, and keep thee: the Lord make His face shine upon thee, and be gracious unto thee: the Lord lift up His countenance upon thee, and give thee peace."

This threefold repetition parallels precisely the apostolic benediction of the New Testament in 2 Corinthians 13:14: "The grace of the Lord Jesus Christ, and the love of God, and the communion of the Holy Ghost, be with you all." Here in Numbers the name of the Spirit is associated with the Father and the Son in the one name of God.

Further, in Isaiah 6:1-3 we read:

"In the year that King Uzziah died I saw also the Lord sitting upon a throne, high and lifted up, and His train filled the temple. Above it stood the seraphims: each one had six wings; with twain he covered his face, and with twain he covered his feet, and with twain he did fly. And one cried unto another, and said, Holy, holy, holy, is the Lord of hosts: the whole earth is full of His glory."

Thus we find another threefold ascription of praise to the one person. Again, in Isaiah 48:16:

"Come ye near unto Me, hear ye this: I have not spoken in secret from the beginning; from the time that it was, there am I: and now the Lord God, and His Spirit, hath sent Me."

Here we find the "Lord" and the "Spirit" and "Me"—the Coming One. As soon as Jesus walked on earth as an individual among men, it was inevitable that the distinctions in the Godhead should be clearly recognized. And there is no Biblical reason for believing in the deity and personality of the Father and the Son, that does not equally establish that of the Holy Spirit.

At Jesus' baptism (Matt. 3:16, 17) the Father's voice announces pleasure in the Son, and the anointing Spirit descends. Here is a clear-cut distinction of the three on one occasion. In the great commission (Matt. 28:19) the baptismal formula has the name of the Spirit placed on an equality with those of the Father and the Son. In Peter's Pentecostal sermon he said:

"Therefore being by the right hand of God exalted, and having received of the Father the promise of the Holy Ghost, He hath shed forth this, which ye now see and hear." Acts 2:33.

And in the chapters under consideration:

"I will pray the Father, and He shall give you another Comforter, that He may abide with you for ever." "The Comforter, which is the Holy Ghost, whom the Father will send in My name, He shall teach you all things, and bring all things to your remembrance, whatsoever I have said unto you." John 14:16, 26.

"When the Comforter is come, whom I will send unto you from the Father, even the Spirit of truth, which proceedeth from the Father, He shall testify of Me." John 15:26.

"Howbeit when He, the Spirit of truth, is come, He will guide you into all truth: for He shall not speak of Himself; but whatsoever He shall hear, that shall He speak: and He will shew you things to come. He shall glorify Me: for He shall receive of Mine, and shall shew it unto you. All things that the Father hath are Mine: therefore said I, that He shall take of Mine, and shall shew it unto you." John 16:13-15.

To this should be added Paul's statement: "Through Him [Christ] we both have access by one Spirit unto the Father." Eph. 2:18. And in Hebrews 10:9-15, the Father wills, the Son works, and the Spirit witnesses.

Concerning this unfathomable mystery we have absolutely no theory to advance. We make no attempt to define or to analyze the Trinity as to nature. It is simply a truth revealed and declared.

## Historical Survey of Perversion

Just a word more, before leaving this division on the *character* of the Holy Spirit. A brief word on the history of the perversion of this truth may be helpful. In the third century, that time of developing apostasies, Paul of Samosatar advanced a theory denying the personality of the Holy Spirit, regarding the Holy Spirit merely as an influence, an exertion of divine energy and power, an influence moving out from God and exerted on men. Then about the time of the Protestant Reformation two men, Laeleus Socinus and his nephew, Faustus Socinus, revived the theory, and many accepted it.

The chilling influence of this concept has told on all the Protestant churches. In our Authorized Version of 1611 the personal pronoun applied by Christ to the Holy Spirit is translated by the neuter *it,* or *itself,* in Romans 8:16, 26. This is an index of the attitude of the time, for Christian people then spoke of the Spirit as "it."

It is significant that the utterances of the Spirit of prophecy were squarely against prevailing sentiment on the part of some of the pioneers of the Advent Movement, who were inclined to this impersonal idea of an influence, and discounted the doctrine of the Trinity. Verily the source of those inspired writings is heaven, and not earth.

Not only was the personality of the Holy Spirit

attacked in those early centuries, but His deity was challenged in the fourth century by Arius, a presbyter of Alexandria. He taught that God was one eternal person, infinitely superior to the angels, and that His only begotten Son exercised supernatural power in the creation of the third person, the Holy Spirit.

The difference between the two heresies, Socinianism and Arianism, lies in the latter's recognition of the personality of the Holy Spirit while denying His proper deity. According to Arius, the Holy Spirit is a created person. If created, then He is not the deity. So much for the personality of the Spirit.

# CHAPTER THREE

ᚐᚉᚐ-ᚉᚐᚉ-ᚉᚐᚉ-ᚉᚐᚉ-ᚉᚐᚉ

# The Mission of the Spirit

And now we turn to the third phase, the *mission* of the Holy Spirit. He has a fivefold office:

1. He first of all reveals Christ as an abiding presence.

2. He reveals God's truth, making it a reality in the inmost being.

3. He is intrusted to bring holiness to man.

4. He testifies of Christ.

5. He glorifies Christ.

But of all the utterances of Jesus, none perplexed the disciples more than this declaration:

"Nevertheless I tell you the truth; It is expedient for you that I go away: for if I go not away, the Comforter will not come unto you." John 16:7.

How it must have staggered them! For three years Jesus had gone in and out among them. They had listened to the music of His words. They had gazed at the wonder of His deeds. Their dearest hopes were centered in Him. But He declares His departure will be their gain. Why? Because in the flesh He could communicate with them only by the outward touch through messages addressed in imperfect human language. It was an external presence and communion.

### Christ's Personal Presence Localized

Furthermore, His presence was localized, limited, and individualized. If in Judea, He was not in Egypt; if in Jerusalem, not in Capernaum. When He had taught His principles, when He had ordained and commissioned His disciples, and had offered Himself once for all, His bodily mission was fulfilled. And His departure was a necessary preliminary to the Spirit's coming, and that coming would be gain.

Better than His bodily presence during the Christian Era, would be His abiding through the Spirit within His followers. Through the Holy Spirit, He has communion and fellowship with innumerable hearts all over the world. Now He is everywhere present with geographical limitations ended. When Christ was on earth He was at a material distance, because outside of men. Through the provision of the Holy Spirit this distance is annihilated. He is infinitely nearer now than when He washed the disciples' feet. Observe this:

"Pentecost brought them the presence of the Comforter, of whom Christ had said, He 'shall be *in* you.' And He had further said, 'It is expedient for you that I go away: for if I go not away, the Comforter will not come unto you; but if I depart, I will send Him unto you.' *Henceforth through the Spirit, Christ was to abide continually in the hearts of His children. Their union with Him was closer than when He was personally with them.* The light, and love, and power of the indwelling Christ shone out through them, so that men, beholding, 'marveled; and they took knowledge of them, that they had been with Jesus.' "—*Steps to Christ,* p. 80. (Italics mine.)

### The Indwelling of the Spirit

The importance of this tremendous truth cannot be overemphasized. Let us reread John 14:16, 17, 21-23:

"I will pray the Father, and He shall give you another Comforter, that He may abide with you for ever; even the Spirit of truth; whom the world cannot receive, because it seeth Him not, neither knoweth Him: but ye know Him; for He dwelleth with you, and shall be *in you.*" "He that hath My commandments, and keepeth them, he it is that loveth Me: and he that loveth Me shall be loved of My Father, and I will love him, and will manifest Myself to him. . . . Jesus answered and said unto him, If a man love Me, he will keep My words: and My Father will love him, and we will come unto him, and make our abode with him."

Through the ages past the Holy Spirit had been *with* men, but from Pentecost forward God's purpose was that He "shall be *in* you." This is to be a sacred reality. The world receives Him not, because it sees Him not. The world's devotion is to the visible, the material. But the Christian is to realize the personal occupancy and indwelling of God the Spirit.

The first and second persons of the Godhead now hold their residence on earth through the third. He is the abiding representative. The presence of the one involves the presence of the others. Thus we are made aware of Christ's presence. To know the Father we must know the Son (Matt. 11:27), and to know the Son we must know the Spirit. So the Son reveals the Father, and the Spirit reveals the Son.

Thus our orphanage ceases. There is no desolation, no loneliness. Men hunger for the personal presence of Christ. And as we yield to the Holy Spirit, we have that transforming presence. Read it:

"The work of the Holy Spirit is immeasurably great. It is from this source that power and efficiency come to the worker for God; and *the Holy Spirit is the Comforter, as the personal presence of Christ to the soul.*"—MRS. E. G. WHITE, in *Review and Herald,* Nov. 29, 1892. (Italics mine.)

### Unites Life of God and Man

The Holy Spirit comes as God to take possession of the life. There is consciousness of the living, glorified Lord. And He will impart Himself to each soul as completely as if he were the only one on earth in whom God dwells. And this intercourse may be unbroken. While the historical Christ is absolutely necessary, yet He does not save from the *power* of sin. We must have a present, living Saviour, the Christ of history becoming the Christ of experience.

Again we read:

"The Holy Spirit seeks to abide in each soul. If it* is welcomed as an honored guest, those who receive it will be made complete in Christ. The good work begun will be finished; the holy thoughts, heavenly affections, and Christlike actions will take the place of impure thoughts, perverse sentiments, and rebellious acts."—*Counsels on Health,* p. 561.

"And shall be in you!" For this, man was created. For this, Jesus lived and died. For want of this, the life of the disciple is honeycombed with failure, while the true Christian life is just Jesus living out His life in us. We are to be charged with the sense of His presence. Henceforth He is the one great glorious living reality, filling the whole horizon.

The Son of man came into the world to unite the very life of God with the human life of man. When He completed His work by His obedience, death, and resurrection, He was exalted to His throne, that the Holy Spirit which had dwelt in Him might come as this all-prevailing sovereign presence, and the disciple becomes the participant of His very life. So the life of the Creator penetrates the life of the

---

* It was after the Minneapolis Conference, and especially as Mrs. White was preparing the chapters for *The Desire of Ages* (1898) concerning the promise of the bestowal of the Holy Spirit, that messages came to this people with increasing frequency, fullness, and clarity on the personality of the Spirit, and His crucial place in the plan of redemption. In earlier statements the neuter form *It* was more often used when referring to the Holy Spirit. The hour had come for clarification and emphasis upon this supreme provision in the salvation and enabling of man.

creatures. Thus we find what the Holy Spirit is doing in us. Note it:

"Transformation of character is the testimony to the world of an indwelling Christ. The Spirit of God produces a new life in the soul, bringing the thoughts and desires into obedience to the will of Christ; and the inward man is renewed in the image of God."—*Prophets and Kings,* p. 233.

### Guides Us Into All Truth

Now He also does this *for* us—He will guide us "into all truth." For He is Himself the "Spirit of truth." (John 16:13.) And He is to teach us "all things." (John 14:26.) There is not a truth we need to know into which the Holy Spirit is unprepared to guide us. And we never get beyond that need.

There was a guide in the deserts of Arabia who was said never to lose his way. He carried in his breast a homing pigeon with a fine cord attached to its leg. When in doubt as to the path to take, he tossed the pigeon into the air, and the pigeon quickly strained at the cord as it tried to fly in the direction of home. So it led its master unerringly home, and people called him the "dove man." Similarly, the Holy Spirit is the heavenly dove, able and willing to lead us if only allowed to do so.

The Holy Spirit is the inner life of truth, the great fact of truth, the living, personal Teacher. Thus we read:

men, is to put the human in place of the divine, and in effect to adopt the Roman Catholic principle.

## Completing the Arrested Reformation

There have been three great movements out of and away from the Papacy—the Reformation of the sixteenth century, headed by Luther; the evangelical revival led by Wesley and his associates; and this last-day message and movement.

Luther's Reformation was necessary, for in the early centuries the Holy Spirit was dethroned and Constantine was made the patron of the church. Through materialistic concepts they lost sight of justification by faith, because they lost their loyalty to the Holy Spirit. So they lost the application of the death of Christ by the Holy Spirit in response to personal faith.

The evangelical revival was necessary because the church of the Reformation had lost its vision of sanctification, and Wesley was raised up to promote holiness. It was hidden because the church failed to heed the Holy Spirit. He is so called, not because holier than the other persons of the Godhead, but because one of His special functions is to cultivate holiness in man. The fox-hunting parsons, so common in the eighteenth century, cared little for God or for the salvation of souls. But Wesley and the Holy Club of Oxford brought forth again the truth of sanctification of human lives for service.

This twentieth-century reformation, or Advent Movement was initiated in the purpose of God to complete these previous, arrested reformations of the past. It calls for the full repudiation of all the perversions introduced by the Papacy and retained by apostate Protestantism on the one hand, and complete restoration of the Holy Spirit to His rightful, sovereign place in belief, life, and service, on the other hand.

It is the full acceptance of this that brings the latter rain, in the time of which we have been living since 1888, but the power of which still largely awaits us.* The inevitable logic of this is unassailable.

How much we need to be awake and alive to meet the situation! Years ago a steamer was making its way down North River at night. The pilot gave a sharp signal to slow up. There was a bright moonlight, and no obstacles ahead. "Why did you ring to slow up?" the engineer asked, as he came on deck to learn the cause. "There is a mist gathering. The night is getting dark, and I—can't—see—the—way," was the pilot's faltering reply. The engineer looked into the pilot's face, and saw that he was dying.

Ah, there is more than one spiritual pilot who is dying spiritually, and cannot see to guide on the true course. God give us new life from the source of life in this treacherous hour.

* See *Christ Our Righteousness*, by Arthur G. Daniells.

≪≪-≪≪-≪≪-≪≪-≪≪

# CHAPTER FOUR

# The Spirit's Work
## for the Unregenerate

SO MUCH for the Holy Spirit's work with the believers. We turn now briefly to His work with the unregenerate world. John 14 deals primarily with the Holy Spirit in the personal life and preparation of the disciple. But John 16 sets forth His work in connection with the worker's public labor and witnessing. In the first He is *in* the believer, and by that indwelling there is union with Christ.

But the Holy Spirit also strives *with* the worldling as the Spirit of conviction. "When He is come, He will reprove the world of sin, and of righteousness, and of judgment: of sin, because they believe not on Me; of righteousness, because I go to My Father, and ye see Me no more; of judgment, because the prince of this world is judged." John 16:8-11.

### Brings New Sense of Sin

The coming of the Holy Spirit brings a new sense of sin to the soul. Think back to the upper room, as the disciples were about to partake of the emblems of the body to be broken and the blood outpoured, yet quarreling over priority of position. This would have been absolutely impossible if they had had a true sense of sin.

There are often incredible things in the lives of Christians, inexplicable except on the basis of a lack of a real sense of the sin involved. Strife for foremost position, envy, malice, evil thinking, impure acts, hatred of one another—these exist principally because of an appalling lack of the sense of sin. But turn to the epistles of Peter, and read the utterances of John after Pentecost. The coming of the Holy Spirit had made real the holiness of God and the utter loathsomeness of sin.

The outlook of the sinner is sin, righteousness, judgment—touching past, present, and future. They are inseparably connected. The Holy Spirit takes these three cardinal facts and places them in their true light. And three persons are involved—man, Christ, and Satan. So here is the heart of the great controversy and the problem of sin.

Conviction of righteousness always precedes the experience of righteousness. And conviction of judgment is indispensable as we present the sanctuary truth and the first angel's message, that men shall stand without excuse, having neglected the testimony of God against themselves.

We are baffled, bewildered, confounded by our utter inability to convince men of sin, righteousness, and judgment. We cannot do it, for that is the Spirit's work. Note it:

"Without the divine working, man could do no good thing. God calls every man to repentance, yet man can not even repent unless the Holy Spirit works upon his heart."—*Testimonies,* vol. 8, p. 64.

This change is wrought by the Spirit:

"None are so vile, none have fallen so low, as to be beyond the working of this power. In all who will submit themselves to the Holy Spirit a new principle of life is to be implanted; the lost image of God is to be restored in humanity.

"But man can not transform himself by the exercise of his will. He possesses no power by which this change can be effected. The leaven—something wholly from without—must be put into the meal before the desired change can be wrought in it. So the grace of God must be received by the sinner before he can be fitted for the kingdom of glory. All the culture and education which the world can give, will fail of making a degraded child of sin a child of heaven. The renewing energy must come from God. The change can be made only by the Holy Spirit. All who would be saved, high or low, rich or poor, must submit to the working of this power."—*Christ's Object Lessons,* pp. 96, 97.

### Brings Conviction of Hope

But notice how—when He is to come *to you,* He will convict the *world!* As, Spirit-filled, we go out into all the world in this hour of the judgment to plead with men, the Spirit will go with us, convincing of sin, and revealing righteousness only in Christ.

He convicts not of unbelief, but of sin through unbelief. He revolutionizes man's ideas of sin—the sin of man and the judgment of God, and the means of escaping by the cleansing blood of Christ and the reigning Spirit within.

And He reveals the atonement provided, thus bringing comfort with conviction. This touches the standard of the law. It involves Sabbath breaking and all other transgressions. Thus the threefold work of Christ as prophet, priest, and King is appropriated by this threefold conviction of the Spirit.

Conscience brings the conviction of despair, while the Holy Spirit brings the conviction of hope. The same wind that tosses the Atlantic into restless heaps, quietly fans it in tranquil calm. Not conscience, but conscience illuminated by the Holy Spirit and the Word, is the world's need.

Not until seated at the right hand of the Father had Christ perfected righteousness for us. He "was delivered for our offenses," He "was raised again for our justification" (Rom. 4:25), and He was enthroned for our assurance. This mission of the Spirit has not been the work of a day. It may seem slow to men, but God is building for eternity; and "whatsoever God doeth, it shall be for ever."

The Holy Spirit's work is to convict men of the terrible sin of rejecting Christ—"of sin, because they believe not on Me." John 16:9. (See also John 3:18.) That is the issue, and it involves all else. The one supreme responsibility of the sinner is the personal rejection of the all-sufficient life and death of Jesus. God has caused man's eternal salvation to hinge on faith in Jesus Christ. This unbelief is the mother of all sin.

### Righteousness the Issue of Salvation

The problem of all human destiny is the attain-ment unto the righteousness of God, for without this no man can stand in the presence of God. (Heb. 12:10, 14.) Christ was made "sin for us," that "we might be made the righteousness of God in Him." 2 Cor. 5:21. This is the issue in salvation, and not merely the question of our outward moral life. And this must be the heart of our message as we lift up the standard and vindicate the downtrodden law of God in this rebellious generation.

How we need the power of the Holy Spirit to give authority to the presentation of the awful truths of final judgment, the inevitable day of wrath impending, and the triumph of righteousness to empower the message of the remnant church! Men go about to "establish their own righteousness" rather than come under the bestowed righteousness of Christ. A divine power is needed.

No human power or argument is sufficient to enlighten a darkened soul concerning the necessary steps into the path of life. And this is the work assigned to the all-sufficient Spirit:

"Even if our gospel is veiled, it is veiled in them that perish: in whom the god of this world hath blinded the minds of the unbelieving, that the light of the gospel of the glory of Christ, who is the image of God, should not dawn upon them." 2 Cor. 4:3, 4, A.R.V.

### Christ's Supreme Gift for Us

Thank God for the Holy Spirit, who has come as the divine substitute, the divine presence, the divine instructor, the divine mentor, the divine testifier, the divine convictor, the divine comforter—Christ's other self.

Did you ever picture what the earth would have been had not the Holy Spirit come? No comfort, no abiding power, the work of Christ of no avail; no conviction of sin, so no repentance and no faith in the Lord Jesus Christ, and no forgiveness of sin; no balm for the troubled conscience, no deliverance from the power of sin, no Teacher and Guide—just orphans, homeless wanderers in a hostile world! The turning point between the darkness and the light in this dispensation was "when the Comforter" came.

Titian, the great painter, met a young soldier with a gift of art that seemed promising. He urged him to give up his military life and devote his talents to painting. This he did, and labored long upon an ambitious painting. But he came to a point where he felt that his genius had failed. In despair, he threw down his brush. Titian found him weeping in despair.

The master artist didn't ask the reason, but going into the studio, realized, as he looked at the painting, that the lad had reached his limit. So Titian took up the brush, and remained at work until he finished the picture.

The next day the young man came to the studio resolved to tell Titian he would try art no more. But as he entered, there on the easel stood the finished picture. That wherein he had failed he saw that a master hand had made up. He knew instinctively that his master had completed it.

With tears of appreciation he said to himself: "I cannot abandon my art. I must continue for Titian's sake. He has done so much for me, I must forget myself and live for him; for now his fame is my fame. He has done his best for me; I will do my best for him." And today his pictures hang side by side with Titian's on the gallery walls of the world.

But, oh, Jesus has done so much more for us than that! Through the Holy Spirit He has done His best for us; and now we must give our best to Him. Then through eternal ages our lives will stand side by side with His life in the eternal gallery of the ages, the Paradise of God.

# Part II

## *The Coming of the Spirit*

# >>>->>>->>>->>> Come, Holy Spirit <<<-<<<-<<<-<<<

COME, Holy Spirit, save me from myself,
   And speak to me each day as friend to friend;
My comfort be in sorrow, pain, and woe,
   From hurtful, lurking foes defend.

Come, Holy Spirit, dwell within my heart;
   Guide Thou my feet to unscaled heights above,
And every impulse of my being thrill
   With holy, pure, and matchless love.

Come, Holy Spirit, with Thy power intrust,
   Else would my toil and labor be in vain;
For whitening fields the reapers now invite,
   As lowly bends the ripening grain.

Come, Holy Spirit, fire my soul with zeal,
   Consuming every trace of selfish dross,
That I may lead my brother lost in sin
   To Calvary's bleeding, cleansing cross.

—B. M. GRANDY.

⟨⟨⟨-⟨⟨⟨-⟨⟨⟨-⟨⟨⟨-⟨⟨⟨-

# The Coming of the Spirit

"THEN opened He their understanding, that they might understand the scriptures, and said unto them, Thus it is written, and thus it behoved Christ to suffer, and to rise from the dead the third day: and that repentance and remission of sins should be preached in His name among all nations, beginning at Jerusalem. And ye are witnesses of these things. And, behold, I send the promise of My Father upon you: but tarry ye in the city of Jerusalem, until ye be endued with power from on high. And He led them out as far as to Bethany, and He lifted up His hands, and blessed them. And it came to pass, while He blessed them, He was parted from them, and carried up into heaven. And they worshipped Him, and returned to Jerusalem with great joy: and were continually in the temple, praising and blessing God." Luke 24:45-53.

"The former treatise have I made, O Theophilus, of all that Jesus began both to do and teach, until the day in which He was taken up, after that He through the Holy Ghost had given commandments unto the apostles whom He had chosen: to whom also He shewed Himself alive after His passion by many infallible proofs, being seen of them forty days, and speaking of the things pertaining to the kingdom of God: and, being assembled together with them, commanded them that they should not depart from Jerusalem, but wait for the promise of the Father, which, saith He, ye have heard of Me. For John truly baptized with water; but ye shall be baptized with the Holy Ghost not many days hence. When they therefore were come together, they asked of Him, saying, Lord, wilt Thou at this time restore again the kingdom to Israel? And He said unto them, It is not for you to know the times or the seasons, which the Father hath put in His own power. But ye shall receive power, after that the Holy Ghost is come upon you: and ye shall be witnesses unto Me both in Jerusalem, and in all Judaea, and in Samaria, and unto the uttermost part of the earth." Acts 1:1-8.

"When the day of Pentecost was fully come, they were all with one accord in one place. And suddenly there came a sound from heaven as of a rushing mighty wind, and it filled all the house where they were sitting. And there appeared unto them cloven tongues like as of fire, and it sat upon each of them. And they were all filled with the Holy Ghost, and began to speak with other tongues, as the Spirit gave them utterance. And there were dwelling at Jerusalem Jews, devout men, out of every nation under heaven. Now when this was noised abroad, the multitudes came together, and were confounded, because that every man heard them speak in his own language. And they were all amazed and marvelled, saying one to another, Behold, are not all these which speak Galilaeans?" Acts 2:1-7.

"We do hear them speak in our tongues the wonderful works of God. And they were all amazed, and were in doubt, saying one to another, What meaneth this? Others mocking said, These men are full of new wine. But Peter, standing up with the eleven, lifted up his voice, and said unto them, Ye men of Judaea, and all ye that dwell at Jerusalem, be this known unto you, and hearken to my words: for these are not drunken, as ye suppose, seeing it is but the third hour of the day. But this is that which was spoken by the prophet Joel: And it shall come to pass in the last days, saith God, I will pour out of My Spirit upon all flesh: and your sons and your daughters shall prophesy, and your young men shall see visions, and your old men shall dream dreams: and on My servants and on My handmaidens I will pour out in those days of My Spirit; and they shall prophesy." Verses 11-18.

"And it shall come to pass, that whosoever shall call on the name of the Lord shall be saved." Verse 21.

"This Jesus hath God raised up, whereof we all are witnesses. Therefore being by the right hand of God exalted, and having received of the Father the promise of the Holy Ghost, He hath shed forth this, which ye now see and hear." Verses 32, 33.

"Therefore let all the house of Israel know assuredly, that God hath made that same Jesus, whom ye have crucified, both Lord and Christ. Now when they heard this, they were pricked in their heart, and said unto Peter and to the rest of the apostles, Men and brethren, what shall we do? Then Peter said unto them, Repent, and be baptized every one of you in the name of Jesus Christ for the remission of sins, and ye shall receive the gift of the Holy Ghost. For the promise is unto you, and to your children, and to all that are afar off, even as many as the Lord our God shall call." Verses 36-39.

‹‹‹-‹‹‹-‹‹‹-‹‹‹-‹‹‹

# CHAPTER FIVE

# The Coming of the Spirit

WHEN Jesus was gathering the dozen men about Him through whom He would found the Christian church, He did not seek them in the venerable schools of the rabbis, or in the exclusive circle of the Sanhedrin. He did not send to Greece, the center of philosophy and culture, for His disciples. Nor did He go to Rome, the home of legislative genius and military prowess, to find His apostles. No, He trod the shining shores of Galilee, and selected humble men whose hearts were big enough to admit the Lord of glory; men who would finally be willing to be nothing that Christ might be everything; men through whom the Holy Spirit could work, unhampered by human sophistry, selfishness, or superiority.

## Wholly Unfitted for Designated Task

Yet to bring them to this essential state of mind and heart was a long and difficult task. Not during Christ's physical, personal stay on earth was it accomplished. For three and a half years they listened to a greater than Solomon. They heard from His own lips the truths of the gospel. They were eyewitnesses of His miracles. To them the inner meanings of His parables were explained. If all that men needed was a Teacher, and lessons of divine wisdom, then the disciples should have been of all men best qualified to carry out the great commission to evangelize all nations immediately upon Christ's ascension.

Yet with all their priceless privileges they were wholly unqualified, as the strife for supremacy, the forsaking, the denial, and the despair so clearly indicate. They were wholly unfitted for their designated task until they had received the great equipment promised. Jesus gave them life, but not power; truth, but not the efficacy of truth, when with them on earth.

For a little time the cross extinguished their hope. They had followed Him whom they loved. Then they saw the detested Romans scourge that blessed back and pierce those holy hands and feet. They were utterly overcome as they saw Him expire on the cross. How sincere was their sad sigh, "We hoped that it was He who should redeem Israel." Luke 24:21, A.R.V. They did not see that His death meant life to them. They did not understand that apparent defeat was the way to victory, and that darkness was the price of light. Even after the resurrection they asked, "Wilt Thou at this time restore again the kingdom to Israel?" Acts 1:6.

They had made no progress. They were still bound by materialism and fettered by national prejudices. They did not understand the Messiah's mission. They dreamed of restoration of the old, whereas He came to inaugurate the new. Their love and confidence were deep and intense. They had forsaken all to follow Him. They knew the resurrection was a glorious fact. Yet they were utterly unfit for their appointed work.

### Doomed to Failure Without Spirit

In handing over the great commission to the apostles after His earthly work was finished and He was ready to take His seat on high, there were three things that were emphasized:

"Jesus came and spake unto them, saying, All power is given unto Me in heaven and in earth. Go ye therefore, and teach all nations, baptizing them in the name of the Father, and of the Son, and of the Holy Ghost: teaching them to observe all things whatsoever I have commanded you: and, lo, I am with you alway, even unto the end of the world." Matt. 28:18-20.

1. The power that they needed was vested in Christ.

2. Therefore they were to "go," teaching all nations, "baptizing" not only into the name of the Father and Son, but also into the name of the Holy Spirit, through whom the power would be applied; and—

3. They were to teach the observance of all things commanded by Christ. But this could be done only through the ministry of the divine Teacher,

Remembrancer, and Guide foretold in John 14:26 and 16:13.

Yet when Christ ascended, He left the disciples in utter impotence amid the deadly enmity of the world. The one thing needful was power from on high, the power of the promised Holy Spirit. And the one thing they were told to do was to wait for the coming of the promised Spirit. How tragically hopeless everything would have been without the promised power. Thus we read Christ's last command: "Behold, I send the promise of My Father upon you: but tarry ye in the city of Jerusalem, until ye be endued with power from on high." Luke 24:49.

"Tarry ye!" until endued, no matter how long it takes. The words were uttered by none other than the same Lord who had just said, "Go ye!" Surely the charge must have caused the most intense surprise, speculation, and expectation. And He was talking to the preachers, teachers, pastors, evangelists, whom He had called and commissioned. "What— tarry longer, with a great perishing world to warn, a tremendous work to do, and a church to upbuild? We have no time to lose. We are belated now." *But they were doomed to failure unless they tarried.*

No one is equipped for gospel service unless and until endued with this heavenly power. Knowledge is not enough; activity is not enough; one must have the power of the Holy Spirit. Not even was the authority to cast out demons sufficient.

### Tarrying Precedes the Going

With increasing seriousness the church is heeding the divine injunction, "Go ye." But it has not yet sensed the solemn necessity of the second mandate, "Tarry ye," which is its inseparable corollary. We are more willing to attempt the first than to obey the second. Yet the same Lord uttered both commands. Note this:

"What we need is the baptism of the Holy Spirit. Without this, we are no more fitted to go forth to the world than were the disciples after the crucifixion of their Lord. Jesus knew their destitution, and told them to tarry in Jerusalem until they should be endowed with power from on high."—Mrs. E. G. White in *Review and Herald,* Feb. 18, 1890.

"The preaching of the word will be of no avail without the continual presence and aid of the Holy Spirit. This is the only effectual teacher of divine truth. Only when the truth is accompanied to the heart by the Spirit, will it quicken the conscience or transform the life."—*The Desire of Ages,* p. 671.

Especially searching is this statement:

"If divine power does not combine with human effort, I would not give a straw for all that the greatest man could do. The Holy Spirit is wanting in our work."—Mrs. E. G. White in *Review and Herald,* Feb. 18, 1890.

The Lord is not in a hurry, though men may be.

God sent Moses into the desert for forty years to fit him for his task, when he was already forty years of age, and the children of Israel were smarting under the lash of the taskmaster and waiting for a deliverer. As in the exodus movement, so in the Advent Movement, God will fit His leaders and ministers before He delivers His people from spiritual Egypt. He sent Paul into Arabia for three years, after the vision of his Lord, preparing him for the first world mission movement, and the ancient world was waiting in darkness. Is less demanded in the last world mission movement?

Jesus spent thirty years preparatory for three and a half years' work. If our sinless Lord did not enter upon His public ministry until He was specifically anointed by the Holy Spirit, how dare fallible, sinful men attempt to win souls without being filled with the Spirit? How dare we rush in to work where Jesus, apostles, and prophets feared to tread?

The same inspired writer, Luke, continues the narrative of his Gospel in Acts 1:4, 5:

"And, being assembled together with them, [Jesus] commanded them that they should not depart from Jerusalem, but wait for the promise of the Father, which, saith He, ye have heard of Me. For John truly baptized with water; but ye shall be baptized with the Holy Ghost not many days hence."

Arthur T. Pierson has aptly suggested that the "Acts" should really be named "The Acts of the

Holy Spirit." Here again they were admonished to "wait" for "the promise." There are many promises in the divine Word. But there is only one that was designated by Jesus as *"the"* promise—standing pre-eminently among all the "exceeding great and precious promises" of our God. And this promise connected the mission of the Holy Spirit with the evangelization of the world.

### Apostolic Vacancy Filled Prematurely

How hard it is to wait! This is exemplified in filling the vacancy made by the treason of Judas. The disciples had had no voice in the choosing of the twelve. Jesus had made the selections personally, and without consulting others. But Jesus had now gone away. He had told the apostles not to take any steps until "the promise" was fulfilled. They were to wait, to tarry until the Holy Spirit came.

But they selected certain names, and proceeded to cast lots upon them before the Lord, and Matthias was declared elected. God does not forsake, even though man is disobedient. He is long-suffering. But evidently Matthias was never the Holy Spirit's real choice. Jesus had gone, the divine Administrator had not yet come, and a valid election was impossible. The disciples should have waited; but they proceeded with the appointment.

Two years later Saul of Tarsus was the one called of God. "Paul, an apostle, (not of men, neither by man, but by Jesus Christ, and God the Father, who raised Him from the dead)." Gal. 1:1. In the foundations of the New Jerusalem, in which are engraved the names of the twelve apostles, the name of Paul will undoubtedly appear as the twelfth.

It is no more possible *rightly* to appoint an officer of the church than to preach a sermon, save by the Spirit of God. Too often there is a show of hands instead of a prayerful waiting for the direction of the Holy Spirit, a substitution of the voice of human choice instead of the voice of the Spirit. But a show of hands is of little value unless they are stretched out toward Him who holdeth the stars of the churches in His hand. (Rev. 2:1.)

### The Paraclete to Choose and Use

A minister is not an accredited messenger of God unless called and anointed by the Holy Spirit. We read:

"Those only who are thus taught of God, those only who possess the inward working of the Spirit, and in whose life the Christ-life is manifested, can stand as true representatives of the Saviour."—*Gospel Workers*, p. 285.

It is His work to appoint *for* service as well as to empower *in* service. In apostolic times the pastors were selected by the Holy Spirit, not simply by suffrage of the people. They simply concurred and recognized the Spirit's call.

"Take heed therefore unto yourselves, and to all

the flock, *over the which the Holy Ghost hath made you overseers,* to feed the church of God, which He hath purchased with His own blood." Acts 20:28.

"As they ministered to the Lord, and fasted, *the Holy Ghost said,* Separate Me Barnabas and Saul for the work whereunto I have called them. And when they had fasted and prayed, and laid their hands on them, they sent them away. So they, being *sent forth by the Holy Ghost,* departed unto Seleucia; and from thence they sailed to Cyprus." Acts 13:2-4.

And there is a divine appointment of offices as well as of persons to fill them.

"He gave some, apostles; and some, prophets; and some, evangelists; and some, pastors and teachers." Eph. 4:11.

Unless the Paraclete chooses and uses and blesses, all is in vain. If there were less diplomacy and more prayer, less manipulating and more pleading, the Holy Spirit would have greater opportunity to indicate His will. For the church or a committee to take upon itself to fill offices according to its own preference and will, is nothing short of an affront to the Holy Spirit. The Jerusalem council was a type of all true councils, and of the decisions we read:

"It seemed good to the Holy Ghost, and to us, to lay upon you no greater burden than these necessary things." Acts 15:28.

It is here to be observed that the Holy Spirit's choice is first.

### Pentecost, Installation Day of the Spirit

Pentecost was the Installation Day of the Holy Spirit as the divine administrator of the church. The Holy Spirit is the true and only vicar of Christ on earth. And the entire administration of the church is committed to Him until Christ returns in glory at the Second Advent. From the day of Pentecost onward He has occupied an entirely new position. But He can fully work only through men who have given Him full possession of their lives, and over whom He is able to exercise absolute control.

This was true in apostolic times, so we read in the Acts of the Apostles, that He selected (13:2), sent forth (13:4), empowered (13:9), sustained (13:52), settled questions (15:28), and forbade (16:6, 7). In 1 Corinthians 12 the thought is iterated and reiterated, that the diversities of gifts in the church are appointed by "one and the selfsame Spirit." (See verses 4-13.) This is His blessed prerogative.

"The wheel-like complications that appeared to the prophet to be involved in such confusion, were under the guidance of an infinite hand. The Spirit of God, revealed to him as moving and directing these wheels, brought harmony out of confusion; so the whole world was under His control."—*Testimonies,* vol. 5, p. 752.

"Wait!" was the command before Pentecost. How hard it is to wait on God! It is easy to think we are losing time if we wait on the Holy Spirit for power. So, too often we go to work *for* God without first receiving an unction *from* God. But there is no use to run before one is sent, no use to labor without unction. Many are in too much of a hurry to wait for the heart preparation supremely needed. We live in the days of multiplying labor, forgetting quality of labor in our anxiety for quantity.

"It is our privilege to take God at His word. As Jesus was about to leave His disciples, to ascend into heaven, He commissioned them to bear the gospel message to all nations, tongues, and peoples. He told them to tarry in Jerusalem till they were endued with power from on high. This was essential to their success. The holy unction must come upon the servants of God. . . .

"This is the very course that should be pursued by those who act a part in the work of proclaiming the coming of the Lord in the clouds of heaven; for a people are to be prepared to stand in the great day of God. Although Christ had given the promise to His disciples that they should receive the Holy Spirit, this did not remove the necessity of prayer. They prayed all the more earnestly; they continued in prayer with one accord. Those who are now engaged in the solemn work of preparing a people for the coming of the Lord, should also continue in prayer. The early disciples were of one accord. They had no speculations, no curious theory to advance as to how the promised blessing was to come. They were one in faith and spirit. They were agreed."—*Gospel Workers,* pp. 370, 371 (1893 ed.)

### Perpetual Activity Our Peril

Our temptation is to perpetual activity, to the exclusion of time needed for prayer, study, and spiritual meditation. We contend that we are tardy with our task. Men are dying, and we face the last crisis; so we work on frenziedly, much like the toiling disciples who labored all night and caught nothing. But in the early gray of the dawn, a few minutes in the direct presence and under the specific direction of the Master filled their erstwhile empty nets.

One is forced to the conclusion that in the case of thousands this foundational principle and direct command is largely ignored. Altogether too few have tarried for the heavenly equipment for Christian service. I am persuaded that this is our colossal blunder. I confess it has been mine. We are not to "go" until we are endued. God can do more through us in five minutes when we are endued than we can do in a week alone. Though true love begins at the cross, all true service begins at our personal Pentecost.

"Legal religion will not answer for this age. We may perform all the outward acts of service, and yet be as destitute of the quickening influence of the Holy Spirit as the hills of Gilboa were destitute of dew and rain."—*Testimonies,* vol. 6, pp. 417, 418.

And notice that the disciples were to wait at Jerusalem, with its babel of voices and its crowded streets—the very city that had crucified their Lord only a few weeks before. It was still hostile in its hatred. It was the very city that had spurned and despised the prophets, and over which Christ had mourned: "O Jerusalem, Jerusalem, which killest the prophets, and stonest them that are sent unto thee; how often would I have gathered thy children together, as a hen doth gather her brood under her wings, and ye would not! Behold, your house is left unto you desolate." Luke 13:34, 35.

It was the last place in the world they would ever think of. It proves that God can bless people anywhere. If they had gone into the quiet country, the mountains of Judea, or the shores of Galilee, out of touch with the crying needs of humanity, they would have been tempted selfishly to remain there, as Peter suggested at the transfiguration, forgetful of a world's desperate need.

### Divine Executive of Godhead

Now we come to the marvelous words of Acts 1:8: "Ye shall receive power, after that the Holy Ghost is come upon you: and ye shall be witnesses unto Me both in Jerusalem, and in all Judaea, and in Samaria, and unto the uttermost part of the earth."

These words were uttered immediately before the ascension, and were followed by the return to

Jerusalem and the seeking of the upper room, where the disciples waited.

Jesus had redirected their thoughts into a new channel moving from Himself as center, and with the new concept of the Holy Spirit as the administrator, or divine executive, of the Godhead in the new dispensation. Their minds were lifted from the earthly and material to the spiritual. It was a world vision that He placed before them, and Pentecostal power comes only on that basis. Their hearts were expanded to include the world.

That is why the power of the Holy Spirit was visited upon the apostolic church in the early rain; and it will come as the latter rain upon the remnant church with the same vision. During the intervening years, when the vision was dimmed, the power of the Holy Spirit has never been seen in its fullness.

On March 29, 1848, for a time no water passed over the vast Niagara Falls. Ice of remarkable thickness formed on Lake Erie. The wind broke it up and caused the great cakes of ice to form a mighty ice dam at the entrance to Niagara River. The water below passed over the falls. The rapids vanished, and history records the phenomenon of a dry Niagara. But under the warm rays of the sun the ice barrier gave way, and the vast power of Niagara flowed on again.

Thank God for the returning power of the latter rain.

CHAPTER SIX

# The Tremendous Transaction
## of Pentecost

UNQUESTIONABLY the word *power* is the key word of the text. Coming from the Greek word *dunamis*—from which we derive dynamic, dynamite, dynamo—it is most vital and suggestive. Only by this *dunamis* can the adamant walls of indifference, sin, formalism, and selfishness be blasted through. Only by the drive of this *dunamis* can come the power that will speed up the wheels of this divinely appointed machinery of the Advent Movement. Only through this *dunamis* are the human wires, that are designed to carry the heavenly current, "alive." Only thus shall we have the needed light, heat, and power to fill the earth with the glory of God.

Think now of three phases: the power needed, the nature of the power available, the purpose for which it is bestowed.

"Come and I will show you the greatest unused power in America," said a businessman to a Christian worker, as he led him to Niagara Falls. "There!" he exclaimed, as he pointed to that mighty torrent with its inherent power.

"No," responded the Christian worker, "the greatest unused power in the world is the Holy Spirit of the living God."

4

True! And that is the power we need—heavenly power, not human, natural, or earthly. Power from outside and above ourselves to achieve what we cannot ourselves accomplish.

### A Fourfold Power Imperative

Those apostles needed a fourfold power: First, *spiritual power* to live a holy life, notwithstanding the fleshly propensities still resident in the flesh. Power to live triumphantly, to serve acceptably, and to win souls. Second, they needed the power of *a new affection and will.* Tremendous forces were arrayed against them. Persecution awaited them. At the place of testing they had forsaken Christ and fled. Third, they needed *intellectual power,* because of their ignorance and inability to understand Christ's mission and their task. And, fourth, they needed *power in service* to accomplish the results at which they were to aim. We need precisely the same power.

The root idea of Christianity is God's men and women carrying on God's work in the power of the Holy Spirit which fits them for service. It is indispensable power, genuine power, incomparable power, obtainable power, personal power, and effectual power. And this power is measured by the Holy Spirit. Indeed, the Holy Spirit is Himself the embodiment of that power.

Christ never spoke of the Holy Spirit as an influence or an attribute, like love or mercy. The Holy

Spirit is a person who desires to live in us, and to make available to us the power resident in Him. It is given not to us but to Him. As we receive Him we are empowered both to will and to work. But we cannot have the power without having the Holy Spirit Himself. He is the dispenser and the agent. He comes, not for me to use, but as an all-powerful Person who desires to use me. The final choice rests with me as to whether I shall limit the power of "the Holy One." (Ps. 78:41.)

Originally God put power in the hands of man, but he lost it through the fall back in Eden. God cannot now intrust us with it. But He has put "all power" in Christ, who administers it through the Holy Spirit. And He bestows it on us in Him. Nor is the power given merely for the asking. There are conditions to be met. We have something to do before we are ready to receive it. This will be considered later. But the laws of power are fixed laws. In the spiritual realm, as in the physical, whenever one obeys the law of power, the power is pledged to operate.

### Not Intellect, Oratory, or Psychology

Think now of the *nature* of the power available. It is not intellectual force, as manifested in mighty eloquence. There were greater orators and more learned men in the audience at Pentecost than was Peter. A man may move his fellows by his eloquence and persuasiveness. But that is not the power indi-

cated. It may be added to gifts of learning or eloquence like Paul's; but it may be given to the unlearned like Peter and John.

The skilled actor and silver-tongued orator can
sway an audience mightily, producing deep emotional
effects or tremendous enthusiasm. Their skill and in-
genuity are admired and coveted by all. But that is
not the power of the Holy Spirit. The glowing fire of
intellectualism can overpower until the effect may
seem supernatural, but intellect and the Holy Spirit
must not be confounded.

The highest reach of human genius falls short of
the lowest degree of this divine power. To electrify
one's hearers is one thing; to bring them truly repentant to the feet of Jesus is quite another. One is in
word only; the other is in the power of the Holy
Spirit.

There is a psychological effect often seen in religious meetings which may seem akin in appearance
to the Spirit's work, but they are as far apart as the
poles. Powerful emotional effects are produced by
fine music and skillful acting. But this is simply a
psychological appeal to the emotions. Let there be
no confusion here. Tears in a church service are not
inherently holier than tears in a Chautauqua program.

Even the religious orator's scintillating phrases,
and logical presentation of divine things, that delights
the hearers and impresses the imagination and the
understanding, may be utterly destitute of the Holy

Spirit's power. It is not mere abstract truth as such, but the power of the Holy Spirit witnessing to the truth, that produces spiritual results.

### Hindering Expedients of the Flesh

Often these expedients of the flesh are a hindrance to the effectual working of the Holy Spirit. The Spirit-filled soul winner is frequently supplanted by the religious orator, who comes in to fill all with himself. This is often reflected in our handbills. Not until all confidence in enticing speech has been put away, can God use the foolish things of the world to confound the wise. Often it is the plainest speech uttered by the humblest instruments that is most markedly used.

Rhetoricians can never teach us the secret of the Holy Spirit's power. Immersion in the Divine Word, and utter abandonment into the hands of God, to be subject solely to His will and swayed by His Spirit, are the one true pathway to spiritual power. Paul learned this lesson. In his masterful oration at Athens he met logic with logic and philosophy with philosophy. But he left no church there, and there is no epistle to the Athenians, whereas there are two addressed to the Corinthian converts.

Coming to them, Paul said significantly, "I determined not to know any thing among you, save Jesus Christ, and Him crucified." 1 Cor. 2:2. Again, we read, concerning our attempts to "manage":

"In the saving of the souls of men, God does all the work, making man His instrument. Man cannot manage the work of God in his own way, for the outward work is vain unless God works with it. Divine power must mingle with human effort, or we cannot be laborers together with God."—MRS. E. G. WHITE in *Review and Herald,* May 6, 1890.

The power of the Holy Spirit is not the power of organization, numbers, or wealth. Much of the visible power of the church today is the result of organized forces. Many a "successful" preacher owes his so-called "success" to sheer perfected business and organizational methods on which the world about is run. His influence and prestige are the result of perfected machinery. And this may involve no spiritual power, though it is not inconsistent with it, for the Holy Spirit works through channels of order and system. But it may be simply ecclesiastical machinery —a religious business enterprise, which the preacher builds.

When human ambition achieves the success, it is precisely the same as if one founded and developed a worldly financial enterprise. Then is the church like the ship of death drifting across the ocean, manned by lifeless forms. Dead men in the rigging, dead men at the helm, dead men in the bunks, drifting in silence across the dismal sea of death. There is many a formal church with a dead man in the pulpit and dead souls in the pews, so far as the vibrant life of the

Holy Spirit is concerned. And the finger from heaven writes, "Thou hast a name that thou livest, and art dead."

Surely there is nothing more unseemly, as one writer puts it, than a dead preacher in the pulpit preaching to dead men in the pews.

### Convicts and Wins to Christ

What, then, is the nature of this power, and how does it operate? The power of the Holy Spirit *convicts of sin*. It makes the hearers see themselves as God sees them. It sends people home, not admiring the preacher, but agitated, troubled, often vowing never to hear him again. Yet they know in their souls that he is right and they are wrong. It is the power of conviction which says to the heart, "Thou art the man." Such preachers are not often popular, but they are powerful. Beware of flattery. The personal power of God arraigns the sinner before the bar of justice, and wrongs are righted and confessions made.

Then the power of the Holy Spirit *lifts up Christ* and makes Him real to the hearers. Some sermons leave a vivid impression of truth. Others leave an imperishable consciousness of the Saviour, not as an idea but as a Person. That is true spiritual preaching.

Again, the power of the Holy Spirit *leads* men to a decision. Not merely do they know something they did not know before; not simply do they have new thoughts and concepts to carry away and reflect upon or feel deeply over; but the power of the Spirit presses to decisive action. This is the test of power.

### Provides Power for Witnessing

Next think of the *purpose* for which the power is bestowed. This enduement of power is for witnessing. Our business is to testify as witnesses, not to argue as lawyers. Nothing is so effective as the simple testimony of an honest witness. The learned eloquence of the attorney must give way before it. And nothing is simpler. It is just telling what we have seen, heard, or experienced. Jesus said, "We speak that we do know, and testify that we have seen." John 3:11.

Yes, a witness must *know* something. The poorest peasant can go into court and say, "I witnessed the deed, and testify to what I saw and heard." A witness's words are written down in black and white. He is guilty of perjury if he tells aught but "the truth, the whole truth, and nothing but the truth." A witness does not keep back testimony. He is mindful of the facts, and faithfully declares them.

Christian witnessing calls for personal experience in the deep things of God. It includes what one knows by the divine revelation of the Word. Personal, experimental salvation is imperative, the realization of the things preached. No man has any right to recommend to others what he has not himself tasted and tested. Some people need something to tell more than they need power to tell it. Too often we preach of things in which we have no personal experience. I earnestly ask: What have you to tell that makes you so eager for God to give you power to tell it?

When Peter told the people to "repent" he had himself repented of his own lying, denial, and profanity at the time of his witnessing. So he witnessed both to the necessity of repentance, and to the power of God to transform the repentant one. He declared, "We are His witnesses of these things." Acts 5:32. Are you and I? Verily, experience lies at the foundation of all true witnessing.

And let us not forget, we are to be witnesses unto Christ—about Him. Many fail here. So we read in Luke 24:46-48: "Thus it is written, and thus it behoved Christ to suffer, and to rise from the dead the third day: and that repentance and remission of sins should be preached in His name among all nations, beginning at Jerusalem. And ye are witnesses of these things."

The witness of the New Testament is concerning Christ: "If we receive the witness of men, the witness of God is greater: for this is the witness of God which He hath testified of His Son." 1 John 5:9. If we accept God's witness concerning Christ, we have the personal witness of salvation: "He that believeth on the Son of God hath the witness in himself: he that believeth not God hath made Him a liar; because he believeth not the record that God gave of His Son. And this is the record, that God hath given

to us eternal life, and this life is in His Son." Verses
10, 11. Then it is our privilege and duty to witness
to others, telling others what we know to be true.
This is the greatest privilege offered to sinners saved
by grace.

### Is the Other Witness

True witnessing is impossible save in cooperation
with the Supreme Witness. The Jewish law required
the testimony of two witnesses. And when Peter
preached, the Holy Spirit was the second and major
witness. As Jesus came to bear witness to the truth, so
the Holy Spirit bears witness only to the truth, and
never to a lie, a perversion, or a distortion.

Thus in God's plan the Holy Spirit is a joint witness with us. And our testimony must be in agree-
ment. "We are His witnesses of these things; and so
is also the Holy Ghost, whom God hath given to
them that obey Him." Acts 5:32. Indeed, we are
not constituted true witnesses until we receive the
power of the Holy Spirit.

The English word *witness* comes from the Anglo-
Saxon *witam,* meaning "I know." One reason for so
little real witnessing is that we know so little of the
Lord Jesus Christ ourselves. We cannot witness if we
have nothing to witness to.

It is of further significance that the Greek word
for *witness* is *martus,* from which we derive the
English word *martyr.* Now, a martyr is one who is
convinced of truth, and manifests it in life and death.

The fires of persecution do not make martyrs; they simply reveal them. The man who is not already a martyr never lays down his life for the truth. The martyrs died, not that they might become martyrs, but because they were martyrs.

The Master did not contemplate disciples especially trained to argue and overcome objection, or for them to depend primarily upon lists of proof texts and methods of personal work, proper as they all are; but in bearing testimony to the reality of the joys of salvation in their own souls. If we are saved from death through the ministry of some physician, we do not need special training to fit us to persuade others to come to him. We need to return more and more to simple, joyous testifying. Such is the primal purpose in the bestowal of the power of the Holy Spirit.

### Days of Waiting Bring Accord

After the ascension the Inspired Record says: "Then returned they unto Jerusalem from the mount called Olivet, which is from Jerusalem a sabbath day's journey. And when they were come in, they went up into an upper room, where abode both Peter, and James, and John, and Andrew, Philip, and Thomas; Bartholomew, and Matthew, James the son of Alphaeus, and Simon Zelotes, and Judas the brother of James. These all continued with one accord in prayer and supplication, with the women, and Mary the mother of Jesus, and with His brethren."

Acts 1:12-14. "And when the day of Pentecost was fully come, they were all with one accord in one place." Acts 2:1.

Pentecost was one of the three great Jewish feasts. It held the central place between the Passover and the Feast of Tabernacles. It was dependent upon the Passover, and was dated some fifty days after that feast. If there had been no Passover, there would have been no Pentecost. Similarly, if there had been no Calvary, the Holy Spirit would not have come.

Picture, if you will, those ten days of waiting between the ascension and Pentecost. The angels' words were still ringing in the disciples' ears. Their Master was to come back visibly, bodily. But until He came the invisible Spirit was to take His place. And Jesus' command to tarry was still fresh and vivid. The "they" referred to were the apostles, certain women, and some of the brethren—one hundred twenty in all.

Yet there were over five hundred brethren who saw the Lord after His resurrection and before Pentecost. (1 Cor. 15:6.) So only about one in four tarried as directed. There may be some encouragement for us in that, in the light of conditions and tendencies of today. If we are looking for the whole church to receive the latter rain, that day will never come. It was an insignificant and humble gathering—a few poor, unlearned fishermen, publicans, and other lowly folk, and some humble but devoted women.

During the ten days just one thing occupied all their hearts and gave courage for the future. The "all" of the text included apostles, disciples, and the other followers assembled. The "in one place" was the transient phase, but the "of one accord" is the eternal condition. The place means nothing today, but the *accord*, or unity, means everything.

And they were "steadfast in prayer." The Holy Spirit came at a prayer meeting. Heart beat with heart, and prayer mingled with prayer. And every recorded instance of receiving the Holy Spirit in the New Testament is preceded by earnest prayer. I am afraid we today are failing right here.

And how earnestly they desired the gift! How keen were their regrets over their previous unfaithfulness! How deep and heartfelt their confessions one to another! How they sensed their utter helplessness and nothingness! As each day passed, they wondered whether the Spirit would come that day. Perpetual occupation may be a greater loss of time than devout waiting. But how they needed the Holy Spirit! Multitudes were dying.

### Like the Roar of a Tempest

The first, second, third, fourth, and fifth days come and go. Why has He not come? The sixth, seventh, and eighth days pass. As the days dragged on, how easy it would have been to criticize! No wonder He had not come, with Thomas among them, with his doubting disposition. And Simon Peter! Just remember his oaths and curses. He could scarcely be trusted. And of course there were the sons of Zebedee, who had actually asked for the two chief seats. They surely were self-seekers and firebrands, veritable "sons of thunder." And then there was Mary Magdalene. Just recall her past. How could the Lord bless?

Oh, it is so easy to turn the searchlight on others instead of on self—around instead of within. We are prone to blame others for our own lack of power. But Pentecost proves that if our repentance is true and deep, no blessing is withheld because of past sins. Thank God for that! Let us then draw together, and draw near to Him. Then the Spirit will come.

The ninth day passed uneventfully. Probably the disciples wondered whether the Father might not fulfill the promise on Pentecost. That must be His plan. The last night was doubtless spent in watching, praising, entreating. At length the day of all days dawned. Momentous day! both for the praying disciples and for the surging crowds without, as well as for millions yet unborn—including us today.

This is the sacred record: "Suddenly there came a sound from heaven as of a rushing mighty wind, and it filled all the house where they were sitting. And there appeared unto them cloven tongues like as of fire, and it sat upon each of them." Acts 2:2, 3. Suddenly there was a sound like the roar of a tempest. It was not like any ordinary wind. It came not from north, east, south, or west, but from heaven. It was not wind, but it had the sound of wind. It was not agitated air, but sound. There was no rushing atmosphere to lift a hair or to fan a cheek.

I repeat; it only suggested wind, but was not wind. This sound as of the hurricane was heard through the city by the multitudes in the early morning hour. (Verse 6, A.R.V.) It settled upon or centered in one place, filling the house where the disciples were gathered. It recalled Jesus' statement to Nicodemus, "The wind bloweth where it listeth, and thou hearest the sound thereof, but canst not tell whence it cometh, and whither it goeth: so is every one that is born of the Spirit."

### Essential Fact of Pentecost

And there appeared "cloven tongues like as of fire." They were forked, divided, luminous, having the color and appearance of fire. *They were not fire, but only appeared as of fire.* Sitting one upon each, they were visible to each person's neighbor, but not to himself.

These two symbols—the rushing wind and the fiery tongues—appealing to the seeing and the hearing, were only temporary manifestations that called attention to the descent of the unseen, unheard Spirit who had come. They were signs calling attention to the power present, but they were not that power. But the eye joined the ear in testifying to its presence.

They were mere accompaniments, and had no value except as signs for the moment, marking the official inauguration of the Holy Spirit as Comforter throughout this dispensation. The essential fact of Pentecost was neither of these symbols, but the coming of the Spirit, who, I would emphasize, was unseen and unheard. The supremely important thing is that the disciples were filled with the Spirit. This essential provision was to remain with the church.

When Nansen started on his Arctic expedition, he took a carrier pigeon with him. After a time he wrote a tiny message and fastened it to the bird. Then he took the pigeon and tossed it into the air. It made three circles, and straight as an arrow it flew for a thousand miles over ice and a thousand miles over water, and at last dropped into the cote at the home of the explorer's wife, and she knew that all was well.

### Heaven's Signal to Earth

So with the coming of the Holy Spirit. It was Heaven's signal to earth that Jesus' sacrifice was accepted of the Father, and that He had taken His place at God's right hand, with His full prerogatives as Heavenly Priest. So all the Spirit's special work for the world during this dispensation found its initial realization and fulfillment at Pentecost.

A new day had dawned in human history, a new departure was initiated in the economy of God, a new era in intercourse between God and man. A new order of things was ushered in at Pentecost, a new relationship of which the Old Testament types and shadows were the whisperings. They were like gleams of early light or songs of hope in the night— visions of glorious coming things now realized.

"When Christ passed within the heavenly gates, He was enthroned amidst the adoration of the angels. As soon as this ceremony was completed, the Holy Spirit descended upon the disciples in rich currents, and Christ was indeed glorified, even with the glory which He had with the Father from all eternity. The Pentecostal outpouring was Heaven's communication that the Redeemer's inauguration was accomplished. According to His promise He had sent the Holy Spirit from heaven to His followers, as a token that He had, as priest and king, received all authority in heaven and on earth, and was the Anointed One over His people."—*Acts of the Apostles,* pp. 38, 39.

The powers of the unseen world were released, and flooded the lives of the disciples in the upper room. There was new life and power in the world. The Holy Spirit had come, not as a temporary visitor, upon some lonely, loyal watcher, but in permanent abiding majesty, to dwell in all yielded lives. Since Pentecost His residence has been on earth, just as Jesus' residence was here during the thirty-three years. Thus was marked the inauguration of a special work to continue until Jesus returns in glory at His Second Advent. So we do not wait for His coming.

### Provisions of Cross Made Effective

The Holy Spirit came to administer the life and power of the risen Christ, and to apply to trusting souls the actual value of the cross, working out in us the consequences of His redeeming work, both as relates to the power and the guilt of sin.

So the coming of the Spirit, making effective the provision of the cross, was the dawn of the brightest day since the fall, to be outshone only by the crowning day when Jesus returns bodily and visibly to reclaim His perfected people who are awaiting translation day, and those whom He calls from their dusty beds. It brought the realization of divine life and power into man's inner life, toward which the plan of God had been moving in the previous dispensation.

There are various ways in which God speaks of this great transaction. He "gives" the Spirit (Luke 11:13; John 14:16), He "sends" (John 15:26; 16:7), He "supplieth" (Gal. 3:5, A.R.V.), He "pours forth" (Acts 2:33, A.R.V.; Joel 2:28), and He puts within (Eze. 36:27). In His coming He proceeded (John 15:26), He "fell" (Acts 10:44), and He descended (John 1:32, 33). In it all there is divine authority, divine grace, divine sovereignty, and divine solicitude.

As the Bethlehem manger was the cradle of Christ, so the Jerusalem upper room was the place of the advent of the Holy Spirit. Pentecost was His installation day in the same way that we speak of that hour in Bethlehem as the birthday of Christ, though both existed before. And in a marvelous sense this is true, for on that day the Holy Spirit began, under new conditions and new manifestations, impossible before, His career in His official capacity as Advocate on earth of our glorified Lord Jesus Christ in heaven.

There was a difference thenceforth in His mission. He came now as the Spirit of Christ, to bring His personal presence to the soul. He understands our needs. He is fully able to succor. He is touched with the feeling of our infirmities. He prays for us with groanings that cannot be uttered in words.

### The Transformation Wrought

What had been promised in the Gospels was experienced in the Acts. The Master's promise was fulfilled to the letter. The disciples were thereby completely changed, and turned the world upside down. Before Pentecost the disciples loved their Lord, but were unable to witness effectually, in the sense Jesus designed. They were devoted but defeated. Afterward cowards became brave, and bosoms that heaved with rivalry and suspicion were filled with humility and love.

Before Pentecost, James and John were narrow and intolerant. When a few timid Samaritans refused to receive their Master, these zealots wanted to wither them with fire. And they were filled with small, unworthy ambition—they wanted the front seats in the kingdom. After Pentecost the low ambition and big-otry were gone. James became the mighty man of prayer, and John the spiritual and lowly one who caught the sweetest whispers of divine love.

Then there was the timid son of Jonas, who cowered like a sheep before the taunting question of a servant girl. But afterward he stood like a lion, and charged upon priest and rabble the murder of the Son of God until the crowd became a reverent congregation, and thousands cried out to God for mercy.

Councils of clever men were unable to withstand the disciples. They were the same men, yet different. Each retained the same characteristics, yet was vastly different. What made the change? There is only one explanation—they were "filled with the Spirit;" they had received the "power from on high."

# CHAPTER SEVEN

ᙦ-ᙦ-ᙦ-ᙦ-ᙦ

# Transformed Preachers of Christ

And what does all this transaction of Pentecost mean and involve? During our Lord's three years of intercourse with the disciples, He spared no pains to teach and train them. He instructed, admonished, and pleaded. He rebuked and exhorted. But in most respects the disciples remained much as they were. And why? Because they had only the outward teachings of an external Christ. And this was not sufficient to redeem them from the power of indwelling sin.

He was working upon them largely by external word and influence when here in the flesh. "But the Comforter, which is the Holy Ghost, whom the Father will send in My name, He shall teach you all things, and bring all things to your remembrance, whatsoever I have said unto you." John 14:26. "I have yet many things to say unto you, but ye cannot bear them now. Howbeit when He, the Spirit of truth, is come, He will guide you into all truth." John 16:12, 13.

### Christ's Indwelling Presence

Through the coming of the Holy Spirit at Pentecost He took up His abode in them as an indwelling presence. He filled the innermost recesses of their being, and became the very life of their lives. Thus the amazing transformation, before unaccomplished, was achieved by the indwelling Christ when the Holy Spirit descended. This glorious fact and provision was the source of all the other blessings that came at Pentecost. Note the gem thoughts:

"It is through the Spirit that Christ dwells in us; and the Spirit of God, received into the heart by faith, is the beginning of the life eternal."—*The Desire of Ages,* p. 388.

"On the day of Pentecost the promised Comforter descended, and the power from on high was given, and the *souls of the believers thrilled with the conscious presence of their ascended Lord.*"—*The Great Controversy,* p. 351. (Italics mine.)

"The inexhaustible supplies of heaven are at their command. Christ gives them *the breath of His own Spirit, the life of His own life.*"—*Gospel Workers,* p. 112. (Italics mine.)

"O my brethren, will you grieve the Holy Spirit, and cause it to depart? Will you shut out the blessed Saviour, because you are unprepared for His presence?"—Mrs. E. G. White in *Review and Herald,* March 22, 1887.

The very Spirit who made the incarnation of Bethlehem possible now dwells in sinful men. This is the only possible explanation of Pentecost. Jesus' earthly stay was *with* men, yet outside of men. Now we have His life *in* us through the Holy Spirit. (John 14:16-18, 20.) The change in cowardly Peter came because the courageous victor, even Jesus Himself, now dwelt in Him. The courage of Jesus was communicated to his soul by virtue of Peter's union with Him. When He took up His abode in John, the love, humility, the self-sacrifice, of the lowly Jesus Himself came into and animated him.

### Same Preachers With New Power

And the change wrought within the disciples fitted them for true and effective service. Their new vision was not simply from without, but was the actual outshining of His life. Before the cross they had associated with the external Christ and were reverent. Now they were comrades with Him through His indwelling life. And this changed their whole outlook and behavior. It was thus they were equipped for their apparently impossible task.

This also is the only real and genuine way to live a victorious, triumphant life, and actually to overcome the power of sin in the daily life while living in the flesh. So many have their eyes fixed on the external, historic Christ of nineteen hundred years ago, and whom we must know, that they fail to realize that Pentecost provided for His dwelling in us and working in us. It is thus that He is made unto us "sanctification," just as His atoning death, preceded by His sinless life, provides for our "justification."

Our glorified, ascended Lord, who lived in the flesh among men, now dwells in men by the Holy

Spirit, imparting the very obedience and characteristics of His own life to them. In this dispensation the Holy Spirit is nearer than merely *with* men; He is *within* them. It is this that makes the difference. Thus the yielded life is brought under the control of the Holy Spirit from within as an abiding Presence.

Then the new commandment can be realized. The spirit and love of Jesus fill the life because He fills it. "That He would grant you, according to the riches of His glory, to be strengthened with might *by His Spirit in the inner man;* that Christ may dwell in your hearts by faith; that ye, being rooted and grounded in love, may be able to comprehend with all saints what is the breadth, and length, and depth, and height; and to know the love of Christ, which passeth knowledge, *that ye might be filled with all the fulness of God."* Eph. 3:16-19.

But be it clearly noted that this is the direct antithesis and antidote of any pantheistic philosophy, or of the rationalistic doctrine of "divine immanence."

To work for God is one thing; but to have God work through us is another. It is one thing to forsake the world to follow Christ; it is quite another to be one in whom the Holy Spirit dwells abundantly with His plenitude of power and grace. Pentecost teaches us that it is not a change of men that is needed but changed men. It is the same old preachers with a new power that will finish our world task. And God cannot do something revolutionary *with* men until

He has first done something revolutionary *for* men through the incoming of the Holy Spirit.

That is why it was necessary for Christ to go away, in order that the Comforter might come and live in us. All His earthly work for them found its fruitage and realization for them at Pentecost. But one step more remains—His glorious bodily return when we shall be like Him, for we shall see Him as He is, with no dimming veil between. Then shall we talk openly to Him with whom we now commune through the Holy Spirit.

### Peter's Message at Pentecost

Note next the effect upon Peter, the burning preacher of Pentecost. An hour before the infilling of the Holy Spirit, he was unfit to witness effectually; now he is fitted. Study his sermon. The apostles and the seventy had preached many a sermon before Pentecost, but the Holy Spirit never saw fit to record a single one of them. But the sermon of Pentecost recorded at length by inspiration is full of importance both as to the true method and the subject matter of preaching, and the results as well.

Observe that Peter *stood up.* That was new and revolutionary; it was different from the rabbis. They sat, while heralds stood to deliver their messages. So the apostles were not merely teachers, but heralds. And then Peter *spoke forth.* He enunciated clearly and correctly, so that all heard and understood.

Peter began with the things they knew and led

them into the unknown. That is the true art of preaching. Yet the sermon was destitute of either logical
argument or rhetorical adornment. It was a simple
statement of great facts to which he gave personal
witness. They seem foolish in their utter simplicity
and weakness; yet three thousand were saved by the
simple recital. The Spirit must equip the preacher,
or his sermon degenerates into lifeless rhetoric and
heartless argument.

We vitiate the power of the Holy Spirit by lean-
ing so much upon our human reasonings. Oh, it is
the divine potency of the Holy Spirit that we preachers need above all else. Of the Holy Spirit, Christ
said three things: "He will convict the *world*"; "He
will guide *you*"; and "He will glorify *Me*." So Peter's
sermon was full of Christ. The Holy Spirit was like
a mighty telescope, as it were, bringing Christ near.
So will every Pentecostal sermon be today, irrespec-
tive of the phase of present truth being set forth.

Of course the cry of "fanaticism" was raised. A
Spirit-filled church or preacher will present to the
world the spectacle of supernatural phenomena. And
such presentations produce wonder, perplexity, and
criticism.

Peter spoke forth burning convictions. There
were no probabilities or suppositions in his discourse,
no theories, no compromises. It was stalwartly courageous. It presented the fact of Jesus, and His perfection of life, His vicarious death, His resurrection and

exaltation, and the pouring forth of *"this."* That four-letter word, T-H-I-S, is the key word of the sermon.

The multitude asked, "What meaneth this?" Verse 12. And Peter answering said, *"This* is that which was spoken by the prophet Joel" (verse 16); and sweeping through the sermon, we reach the climax in verse 33: "Therefore being by the right hand of God exalted, and having received of the Father the promise of the Holy Ghost, He hath shed forth *this,* which ye now see and hear." The "this" included all that they had both seen and heard, and which had caused their perplexity. Linking with prophecy, he led directly to the ministration of Christ.

### Convicting, Converting Power

Then were men "pricked in their heart," and "three thousand souls" were added to the Lord. It was not the outflow of human energy, zeal, logical argument, wisdom, or eloquence. No advertising or organizing power accounted for their crowds and results. It was the convicting, converting power of the Holy Spirit. It was the declaration of the Lordship of Jesus, in the power of the Spirit, backed by personal witnessing to the reality.

It produced conviction and inquiry, instruction and exhortation, obedience and addition to the church. That called for the Holy Spirit, now poured out upon "all flesh." That sweeps in the whole race. It cannot be narrowed to anything smaller than the

entire human family. And we are indeed among the
"far-off" ones of verse 39: "The promise is unto you,
and to your children, and to all that are afar off, even
as many as the Lord our God shall call."

As to the results of Pentecost, there was first a
witnessing, then opposition; soon an outbreak of persecution, and later martyrdom for many. Persecution
scattered them from centralization. The same will
come to us. Pentecost brought a new constraint and
a new conviction. It cleared up misconceptions. There
was a great wave of every-member evangelism that
spread out from Jerusalem. Disciples went everywhere preaching the Word. The persecution transformed them into missionaries. Means flowed into
the treasury. It is my conviction that the same process
will be repeated with us.

"Selling their houses or their lands, they brought
the money, and laid it at the apostles' feet, 'and dis-
tribution was made unto every man according as he
had need.' This liberality on the part of the believers
was the result of the outpouring of the Spirit."—*Acts
of the Apostles,* p. 70.

Such was the recital of the early rain.

### Latter Rain to Surpass Pentecost

Under the downpour of the latter rain these
things will be not only paralleled but surpassed.
Mighty things will happen, and that speedily. Power
is always manifested in action. That is the law of

power. May God quickly bring this holy action to cut short and finish the work in righteousness.

When Christ was on earth He spoke to the dead and called them back to life. But I am persuaded that it is an even greater thing to influence successfully a living man's stubborn will that is set against God. It is a greater miracle to quicken spiritually a sinning, God-hating man than to quicken the physically dead. That is undoubtedly what Jesus meant when He declared to His astonished disciples, "Greater works than these shall he do." John 14:12.

That was the miracle of Pentecost, as three thousand souls, filled with prejudice, malice, bitterness, their hands dripping with the blood of Jesus, repented and crowned Him both Lord and Christ.

"These scenes are to be repeated, and with greater power. The outpouring of the Holy Spirit on the day of Pentecost was the former rain, but the latter rain will be more abundant. The Spirit awaits our demand and reception. Christ is again to be revealed in His fullness by the Holy Spirit's power."—*Christ's Object Lessons,* p. 121.

"To us to-day, as verily as to the first disciples, the promise of the Spirit belongs. God will to-day endow men and women with power from above, as He endowed those who on the day of Pentecost heard the word of salvation. At this very hour His Spirit and His grace are for all who need them and will take Him at His word."—*Testimonies,* vol. 8, p. 20.

Thousands of voices give the final warning:

"The great work of the gospel is not to close with less manifestation of the power of God than marked its opening. The prophecies which were fulfilled in the outpouring of the former rain at the opening of the gospel, are again to be fulfilled in the latter rain at its close. Here are 'the times of refreshing' to which the apostle Peter looked forward when he said, 'Repent ye therefore, and be converted, that your sins may be blotted out when the times of refreshing shall come from the presence of the Lord; and He shall send Jesus.'

"Servants of God, with their faces lighted up and shining with holy consecration, will hasten from place to place to proclaim the message from heaven. By thousands of voices, all over the earth, the warning will be given. Miracles will be wrought, the sick will be healed, and signs and wonders will follow the believers. Satan also works with lying wonders, even bringing down fire from heaven in the sight of men. Thus the inhabitants of the earth will be brought to take their stand."

This is all under the conviction by the Spirit:

"The message will be carried not so much by argument as by the deep conviction of the Spirit of God. The arguments have been presented. The seed has been sown, and now it will spring up and bear fruit."—*The Great Controversy*, pp. 611, 612.

《《-《《-《《-《《-《《-

# CHAPTER EIGHT

# The Empowering
## of the Remnant Church

THROUGHOUT the apostolic era the triumphs of the cross continued. The Lord was "working with them, and confirming the word with signs following." Mark 16:20. Idolatry was shattered, pagan temples were emptied, and converts multiplied by the thousands. Without money they overcame the combinations of wealth about them; without schools they put to confusion the learned rabbis; without political or social powers they proved stronger than the Sanhedrin; without a priesthood they defied priest and temple; and without a soldier they were mightier than the legions of Rome. And so they planted the cross above the Roman eagle.

### A Hierarchy Supplants the Holy Spirit

But new privileges bring new responsibilities, and new responsibilities create new perils. The early church gradually forgot the secret stairway to the upper room. By the fourth century the Christian church had transferred her dependence from divine power to the smiles of royalty and the patronage of an earthly throne. She placed henceforth her dependence upon men, methods, and money. The rule and authority of the Holy Spirit was ignored, and the church plunged into the midnight of the Dark Ages. In the great apostasy a hierarchy developed, and at last the usurping head set himself up instead of the Holy Spirit as the vicar of the Son of God, and became the one "who opposeth and exalteth himself above all that is called God, or that is worshipped; so that he as God sitteth in the temple of God, shewing himself that he is God." 2 Thess. 2:4.

The church passing under this dismal eclipse of the Dark Ages was aroused by the trumpet voice of Martin Luther. Little by little the return has been made through the past three centuries, the Holy Spirit being again given His rightful place, until today we stand in the time of the complete and final reformation and the latter rain.

Without controversy the greatest need in the world today is a Spirit-born, Spirit-called, Spirit-filled, Spirit-led ministry to lead the Advent Movement to the finishing of its allotted task. And through the grace of God, what ought to be, may be; and what may be, must be. But the apostasy of the Middle Ages and the loss of the Spirit need not have been.

Note this statement:

"I saw that if the church had always retained her peculiar, holy character, the power of the Holy Spirit which was imparted to the disciples would still be with her. The sick would be healed, devils would be rebuked and cast out, and she would be mighty and a terror to her enemies."—*Early Writings,* p. 227.

## Spirit to Return in Full Power

Pentecost did not exhaust the prophecy of Joel. There is to be a far more complete fulfillment in these last days of the dispensation of the Spirit. What we need is a clear apprehension of the person and work of the Holy Spirit, and a complete surrender to His control. The Spirit of truth, grieved and driven away by apostasy, perversion, and rejection, will return in full power to the remnant church that is seeking to know and obey the full truth.

The apostolic generation (A.D. 31-64), in which the gospel went to the known world, is a type of this last generation of the gospel era, when under the latter rain the "everlasting gospel" goes to the whole world in final consummation. What a solemn and yet glorious time this is in which to live!

"I saw that this message will close with power and strength far exceeding the midnight cry. Servants of God, endowed with power from on high, with their faces lighted up, and shining with holy consecration, went forth to proclaim the message from Heaven. Souls that were scattered all through the religious bodies answered to the call, and the precious were hurried out of the doomed churches, as Lot was hurried out of Sodom before her destruction. God's people were strengthened by the excellent glory which rested upon them in rich abundance, and prepared them to endure the hour of temptation."—*Ibid.,* pp. 278, 279.

5

The work of the whole church is to give the whole gospel to the whole world in this generation. It has no other legitimate business. This is the focal point toward which all history has been unfolding, the objective for which the whole universe is waiting. Under Pentecost the disciples started out to fill the whole world with the gospel. We could not have the latter rain without undertaking a corresponding task. The record of Pentecost fills us with both hope and shame. We absolutely must have Pentecostal power to finish our task. It is the need of all needs. More than that, it is the only hope of the Advent Movement. And the church must return to Pentecost before Pentecost will return to her.

### Greatest Lack of Remnant Church

The Holy Spirit is the church's all-sufficient equipment. So complete was it that with one hundred and twenty Spirit-filled apostolic members there was a greater extension than has ever been made in a like period since that time, all our facilities notwithstanding. And thus we are forced to the conclusion that the remnant church lacks and supremely needs the power of the Holy Spirit that was promised to fit her for her final work.

Men, gifts, methods, legislation, are all dead machinery unless vitalized and made effective by the spirit of Pentecost. The prophet may preach to the bones in the valley but it takes the breath from heaven to cause them to live. Our great lack is not more earnestness, more importunity, more strength, more activity; it is our indifferent attitude toward the Holy Spirit.

We are trying to render acceptable service in neglect of the one power by which it is accomplished. In the church, as in the world, all is rush, speed, pressure. We are so busy that we have no time left for the most needful thing. Our hands are full, but our hearts are too often empty. "The missionary *movement* is far in advance of the missionary *spirit.*" —*Historical Sketches,* p. 294. If we deplore the limitations of our activity, ought we not to be more concerned over our deeper need?

The church is up to date. She has a wonderful organization. She has a marvelous machinery. The wheels are adjusted to a nicety. But she lacks power. In spite of all our facilities, we do not have the power of conversion which should mark the remnant church. We are faltering in the conflict with worldliness, unbelief, and unrighteousness. While the church is evangelizing the world, the world is secularizing the church. Thus her efforts are neutralized. To attract and interest people, ministers are resorting to worldly methods that are miserable makeshifts for the power from on high. It is humiliating to think of some of these worldly expedients used—and so unnecessarily.

Today the world is covered by our missionary

activities. But there is a distressing want of proportion between our activities and our gifts, and the net results, in most sections. Each passing year sees a rising cost for each soul won, coupled with a decreasing return in souls per laborer. This ought to startle us, yes, to alarm us.

Why so little fruit from so great an army? Ah, our relation to the Holy Spirit is too largely unrecognized—and this in His own dispensation. Where are the men filled with the Holy Spirit as were men in apostolic days? We are in gravest peril of depending on men, methods, and money, instead of on Him who alone can raise up men, direct and vitalize them, equip them with right methods, and release and bless the money needed.

### Personal Pentecost Our Birthright

As there was a historic Bethlehem where the Word was made flesh, so there is a personal Bethlehem when Christ is formed within the heart through the Holy Spirit. Similarly, there was a historic Pentecost when the Spirit was poured out upon the church, but there is also a personal Pentecost when He fills the individual believer. And this personal Pentecost is the birthright of every child of God. Alas, many are living experimentally on the other side of Pentecost. But let us not be deceived into looking for the latter rain for ripening, until the early rain has first watered our own individual souls.

Let us read thoughtfully and prayerfully these statements from the Spirit of prophecy:

"The latter rain, ripening earth's harvest, represents the spiritual grace that prepares the church for the coming of the Son of man. But unless the former rain has fallen, there will be no life; the green blade will not spring up. Unless the early showers have done their work, the latter rain can bring no seed to perfection."—*Testimonies to Ministers,* p. 506.

"Many have in a great measure failed to receive the former rain. They have not obtained all the benefits that God has thus provided for them. They expect that the lack will be supplied by the latter rain. When the richest abundance of grace shall be bestowed, they intend to open their hearts to receive it. They are making a terrible mistake. The work that God has begun in the human heart in giving His light and knowledge, must be continually going forward. . . . But there must be no neglect of the grace represented by the former rain. Only those who are living up to the light they have, will receive greater light. Unless we are daily advancing in the exemplification of the active Christian virtues, we shall not recognize the manifestations of the Holy Spirit in the latter rain. It may be falling on hearts all around us, but we shall not discern or receive it. . . .

"The blessings received under the former rain are needful to us to the end. Yet these alone will not suffice. While we cherish the blessing of the early rain, we must not, on the other hand, lose sight of the fact that without the latter rain, to fill out the ears and ripen the grain, the harvest will not be ready for the sickle, and the labor of the sower will have been in vain. Divine grace is needed at the beginning, divine grace at every step of advance, and divine grace alone can complete the work. . . . If we do not progress, if we do not place ourselves in an attitude to receive both the former and the latter rain, we shall lose our souls, and the responsibility will lie at our own door." —*Ibid.*, pp. 507, 508.

As the Holy Spirit came at Pentecost, after the enthronement of Christ in heaven, so it is not until Christ is enthroned King in the individual heart that the personal Pentecost comes. This is our greatest individual need, and therefore our greatest collective need.

Part III

*The Filling of the Spirit*

# ➤➤➤➤➤ *Heavenly Power* ⬅⬅⬅⬅⬅

How oft the power of words prevails,
  Instead Thy word of power;
How oft we turn to human strength,
  When in that very hour
    Thy mighty word,
    That word of God,
In all its truth should tower!

How prone we are to look for force
  Within our words and aims,
And then expect these human plans
  To serve the latter rains—
    The Spirit's gift,
    That gift of God,
Which ev'ry doubt explains!

How much Thy Spirit longs to do
  These stagg'ring tasks we face,
O'er which we wrestle in our strength,
  And fail oft in disgrace!
    Help us to feel
    Our need of Thee,
And all Thy power embrace!

Lord, save us from these carnal ways,
  Reveal Thy Spirit's might;
Thy boundless store of help divine
  To turn men to the light—
    The light of God,
    That light from heav'n
That penetrates earth's night!

—LOUISE C. KLEUSER.

[Written during the meetings of the Spirit-blessed Atlantic Union Ministerial Institute, this poem came into being as an individual response to the messages presented.—L. E. F.]

《《-《《-《《-《《-《《

# The Filling of the Spirit

"A CERTAIN Jew named Apollos, born at Alexandria, an eloquent man, and mighty in the scriptures, came to Ephesus. This man was instructed in the way of the Lord; and being fervent in the spirit, he spake and taught diligently the things of the Lord, knowing only the baptism of John. And he began to speak boldly in the synagogue: whom when Aquila and Priscilla had heard, they took him unto them, and expounded unto him the way of God more perfectly. And when he was disposed to pass into Achaia, the brethren wrote, exhorting the disciples to receive him: who, when he was come, helped them much which had believed through grace: for he mightily convinced the Jews, and that publickly, shewing by the scriptures that Jesus was Christ.

"And it came to pass, that, while Apollos was at Corinth, Paul having passed through the upper coasts came to Ephesus: and finding certain disciples, he said unto them, Have ye received the Holy Ghost since ye believed? And they said unto him, We have not so much as heard whether there be any Holy Ghost. And he said unto them, Unto what then were ye baptized? And they said, Unto John's baptism.

137

Then said Paul, John verily baptized with the baptism of repentance, saying unto the people, that they should believe on Him which should come after him, that is, on Christ Jesus. When they heard this, they were baptized in the name of the Lord Jesus. And when Paul had laid his hands upon them, the Holy Ghost came on them; and they spake with tongues, and prophesied. And all the men were about twelve. And he went into the synagogue, and spake boldly for the space of three months, disputing and persuading the things concerning the kingdom of God." Acts 18:24-28; 19:1-8.

"Wherefore he saith, Awake thou that sleepest, and arise from the dead, and Christ shall give thee light. See then that ye walk circumspectly, not as fools, but as wise, redeeming the time, because the days are evil. Wherefore be ye not unwise, but understanding what the will of the Lord is. And be not drunk with wine, wherein is excess; but be filled with the Spirit; speaking to yourselves in psalms and hymns and spiritual songs, singing and making melody in your heart to the Lord; giving thanks always for all things unto God and the Father in the name of our Lord Jesus Christ." Eph. 5:14-20.

᚛᚛᚛᚛᚛᚛

# CHAPTER NINE

# The Filling of the Spirit

EPHESUS was a city of Lydia on the west coast of Asia Minor. It was situated at the junction of the natural trade routes, about a mile from the Icarian Sea. It was the meeting point of great roads. Its harbor was partly silted up; but still it was thronged with vessels from every part of the civilized world. Its seas and rivers were filled with fish, and its commercial position was unrivaled. Its population was great, and its thronging markets were the Vanity Fair of Asia.

Its inhabitants were ardent devotees of pleasure. It had a giant theater 495 feet in diameter, with a stage 22 feet wide, an orchestra of 110, and 66 rows of seats to accommodate 24,500 persons. It possessed a far-famed religious shrine for the worship of Diana. And commercial and religious interests blended and centered in this temple.

## Apollos' Feeble Ministry

To this important metropolis came Apollos, an Alexandrian Jew who had become a Christian. Alexandria was a center of Greek learning and culture, in which Philo was the outstanding figure. Incidentally, the influence of the Greek mode of thinking had invaded the Hebrew method of studying their own Scriptures. This background is helpful as we turn our thoughts to Apollos.

He was a learned and eloquent man, and was mighty in the Scriptures. He knew how to present them convincingly, and was careful in his teaching. He was gifted in the art of oratory and bold in utterance. He was earnest and fervent in spirit, possibly having imbibed this intensity from John the Baptist. He "taught accurately the things *concerning* Jesus." Acts 18:25, A.R.V. But his presentations were theoretical. And he could take the people only as far as he had gone—not a yard beyond, nor a foot above. There were two humble laymen—Aquila and Priscilla—who knew Jesus better than he, for they knew Him experimentally. These instructed him more fully.

One might think that Apollos would have turned the city of Ephesus upside down through his eloquence, but very little is recorded concerning his ministry, despite the burning eloquence of this sincere soul. There was but little result from his strenuous labor, and he passed on to Corinth. Paul, later coming to Ephesus, sought out the church, and was rewarded with the discovery of only twelve weak disciples. Doubtless they were meeting in some obscure room, exercising but little influence in that vast, idolatrous city, from out of which the grace of God had drawn them.

### Paul's Penetrating Question

Paul saw instantly that there was something lacking in their life and witness. He was convinced that there was a reason why they exercised no greater power. He was a penetrating observer, and he was looking for the cause that produced this effect. Their unsatisfactory condition was pitiably apparent. The poverty of their living Christian experience, the barrenness of spontaneous activity, and the powerlessness of their testimony could not be hidden.

The twelve men represented the product of their eloquent leader Apollos. If a preacher begins with mere eloquence, he usually ends with mere instruction. Too often the divine dynamic will be lacking; for a man can lift others only to the level on which he himself lives.

"The preaching of the word will be of no avail without the continual presence and aid of the Holy Spirit. This is the only effectual teacher of divine truth. Only when the truth is accompanied to the heart by the Spirit, will it quicken the conscience or transform the life. One might be able to present the letter of the word of God, he might be familiar with all its commands and promises; but unless the Holy Spirit sets home the truth, no souls will fall on the Rock and be broken.

"No amount of education, no advantages, however great, can make one a channel of light without the co-operation of the Spirit of God. The sowing of the gospel seed will not be a success unless the seed is quickened into life by the dew of heaven. Before one book of the New Testament was written, before one gospel sermon had been preached after Christ's ascension, the Holy Spirit came upon the praying apostles. Then the testimony of their enemies was, 'Ye have filled Jerusalem with your doctrine.'"—*The Desire of Ages,* p. 671.

Without preliminaries Paul went directly to the crucial point. "Did ye receive the Holy Spirit when ye believed?" he asked. Acts 19:2, A.R.V. And their reply was, "Nay, we did not so much as hear whether the Holy Spirit was given." The disciples of John knew of the Holy Spirit to come, but had not yet received Him. Yet this experience at Ephesus was twenty years after Pentecost.

Paul was not asking concerning the special gifts of the Spirit, but of the *Gift supreme*—the *Holy Spirit Himself.* And their reply indicates that they so understood him. He wanted to learn whether they had received the filling of the Holy Spirit—the permanent, central feature of Pentecost. For there is an experience beyond and above the initial step by which the Holy Spirit first reveals sin, and begets a new life in the soul, and that is *to be filled with the Spirit.* For the lack of this, one's testimony is feeble and the spiritual life but partial.

It is one thing to know something of the Holy Spirit's operations; but a vastly different thing to receive Him as a personal, indwelling Guest. And these Ephesian disciples were still unacquainted experimentally with this great fact and provision. So Paul at once made them conversant with the gospel of the risen and ascended Lord, who was glorified and had received the promise of the Spirit from the Father, which He in turn had sent down into the world for every believer to receive. And then they received the Holy Spirit in harmony with Heaven's provision.

### No Compensation for Spirit's Lack

Alas, many today have gone as far as the baptism of repentance, but no farther. They are honest, sincere, and obedient to the extent of their knowledge. But they are ignorant of the fuller, brighter, larger life. Whatever knowledge they have of the Holy Spirit is vague, indefinite, inadequate. His personality, power, and presence are not understood. They are largely ignorant of His program and provisions, and are sadly barren of His fruits.

It is easy to look back to the cross as the basis of faith, or forward to the throne which we anticipate with hope. But we live in the tremendous present with its terrific problems. And thousands have not yet grasped with any personal appreciation and appropriation the supreme *fact* and *reality* of the Holy Spirit. We are in weakness because the greatest of God's provisions for this dispensation is covered with unreality. We understand other truths, but have not laid hold of this one: that the one supreme fact and force and need in the world today is the Holy Spirit, not merely in the world or church in general, but in the individual life.

So long as ministers imagine that what is needed is just more earnestness, importunity, brilliance, or strength, which if they can only obtain they will be all they ought to be, then their preaching is of little avail, for they are only perpetuating the condition of powerlessness.

As we look back across the centuries to the Ephesus episode, Paul's question suggests the reason why so many lives are spiritual failures and why the church is so feeble. Nothing can compensate for the lack of the Holy Spirit. What steam or gas is to the engine, what electricity is to the motor, that and more is the Holy Spirit in the soul's battle with sin, and in the problem of successful service.

### As Fire Differs From Water

Paul's question marks the boundary line between two classes in the Christian church—those who know Jesus only as a *Saviour,* who forgives their sins and gives them a hope of heaven, and those who know Him as *Lord* over the power of sin, who abides in the soul of the worker as a living presence and personal reality, thus equipping him for fullest service.

Some come with a ministry of repentance, baptizing with water unto an outward cleansing and moral reformation. They virtually make the work of the church moral instead of spiritual, and its primary concern with conduct rather than with the nature, thus dealing with reform rather than inner transformation. But John told of Him who should baptize "with the Holy Ghost, and with fire." His work differs from the simple baptism of repentance, as fire differs from water. It has a power that is internal, consuming, almighty.

It is this that completes the preliminary baptism of repentance. To receive this is "the greatest and most urgent of all our needs." After three years of personal companionship with the disciples, Jesus said it was "expedient" for Him to go away that they might receive the Holy Spirit. The presence of the Spirit, He declared, would be of more value to them than even the continued bodily presence of Himself.

### Powerless Preaching the Result

Again, *whose business is it to raise such a question* as, "Did ye receive the Holy Spirit when ye believed?" Is it not the minister's? Paul did it, and did it promptly when the need was apparent. His question indicated that there had been but a partial instruction. Their lack was primarily the fault of the preacher. That gospel presentation is not complete and adequate which does not set forth the glorious provision of the

Holy Spirit. One partially instructed can have only a partial experience. *But in all too many instances intellectual assent to a gospel of truth has been substituted for this divine provision.*

There are many preachers with wonderful gifts, full of zeal, mighty in the Scriptures, and eloquent, but who leave behind weak, defective converts because they themselves are living experimentally on the wrong side of their personal Pentecost. One cannot give a clear expression unless he himself has a clear impression. The tendency is ever toward the formal, the materialistic, the utilitarian.

It is so easy for the spiritual vision to grow dim. But it is the absence of the Spirit that makes a strong man's preaching powerless. Learning, talent, and eloquence are powerless without the Spirit's presence. If Paul's soul burned as he asked those twelve men that vital question, what would he not say if he could see the church today in this "time of the latter rain"? Observe these searching statements:

"It is the absence of the Spirit that makes the gospel ministry so powerless. Learning, talent, eloquence, every natural or acquired endowment, may be possessed; but, without the presence of the Spirit of God, no heart will be touched, no sinner won to Christ. On the other hand, if they are connected with Christ, if the gifts of the Spirit are theirs, the poorest and most ignorant of His disciples will have a power that will tell upon hearts. God makes them channels for the outflowing of the highest influence in the universe."—*Testimonies,* vol. 8, pp. 21, 22.

"Without the Spirit of God a knowledge of His word is of no avail. The theory of truth, unaccompanied by the Holy Spirit, can not quicken the soul or sanctify the heart. One may be familiar with the commands and promises of the Bible; but unless the Spirit of God sets the truth home, the character will not be transformed. Without the enlightenment of the Spirit, men will not be able to distinguish truth from error, and they will fall under the masterful temptations of Satan."—*Christ's Object Lessons,* pp. 408-411.

"The sword of the Spirit, which is the word of God, pierces the heart of the sinner, and cuts it in pieces. When the theory of the truth is repeated without its sacred influence being felt upon the soul of the speaker, it has no force upon the hearers, but is rejected as error, the speaker making himself responsible for the loss of souls."—*Gospel Workers,* p. 253.

"We are not to make less prominent the special truths that have separated us from the world, and made us what we are; for they are fraught with eternal interests. God has given us light in regard to the things that are now taking place, and with pen and voice we are to proclaim the truth to the world. But it is the life of Christ in the soul, it is the active principle of love imparted by the Holy Spirit, that alone will make our words fruitful."—*Ibid.,* p. 288.

# CHAPTER TEN

≪≪≪≪≪≪

# The Divine Command and Provision

SOME ten years after the events referred to in the last chapter, writing to the larger church at this same city of Ephesus, Paul joins to his original question this solemn injunction: "Be not drunk with wine, wherein is excess; but *be filled with the Spirit.*" Eph. 5:18. Here is a call to receive something. Some were not filled, and their condition brought forth this double injuction, with a negative side and a positive.

It is more than desirable; it is indispensable. It is not merely permissive, but mandatory. One has no more license to break the second part than the first, for one is just as binding as the other. It is more than mere counsel; it is a plain command of universal application, as peremptory as the prohibition against drunkenness. For the believer not to be "filled" is just as much disobedience as for an impenitent sinner not to yield in "repentance" to the will of God.

It is more than a privilege, it is a distinct duty, and is the Christian's birthright. Believing the truth is no substitute. Studying the Bible is no substitute. Intensive activity is no substitute. Keeping the Sabbath is no substitute. We disobey at our peril this positive command enjoined.

## Not by Measure but in Fullness

Think intensively of those words "be filled" for a moment. They are in the present tense, not something we are bidden to look back to. Yes, "be filled." We can be—morning, noon, and night, moment by moment.

"Morning by morning, as the heralds of the gospel kneel before the Lord and renew their vows of consecration to Him, He will grant them the presence of His Spirit, with its reviving, sanctifying power. As they go forth to the day's duties, they have the assurance that the unseen agency of the Holy Spirit enables them to be 'laborers together with God.' "—*Acts of the Apostles,* p. 56.

Unbelief must not say, Such an experience is too high. It is God's command, and therefore as obligatory as any other. Since all God's commands are enablings, they are each tantamount to a promise. We appropriate the other doctrines, exhortations, and teachings of this epistle to the Ephesians; why minimize or omit this one?

All the children of God are *born* of the Spirit; but it is another thing to be *filled* with the Spirit. It is one thing to *have* the Spirit in a measure, or by measure; but quite another for *Him to have us fully.* What He wants is to come in and fill every part of the being. If we have faith to believe that Jesus Christ can save a person from the *guilt* of sin, ought we not to believe that He will fulfill this promise? One is as sacred as the other. One presents no greater impossibility than the other. And the one who has been saved ought to be filled, for Christ's *power* is as available as His *pardon.* To put it succinctly, we are to believe and be saved, and believe and be filled.

Think not it was simply for apostolic times. It is for all who are "afar off" as well. (Acts 2:39.) It is as much for us in the golden glories of time's last hour as for those who lived in the silver dawn of this dispensation of the Spirit.

### Communication of Life to the Soul

"Filled with the Spirit" is contrasted with the exciting influence of alcoholic stimulants. At Pentecost the disciples were charged with being drunken. But the action of the Holy Spirit is here put in contrast with the unnatural, alcoholic state of the drinker. For when the Spirit fills a man, the yielded life is under the direction and control of a divine and supernatural agent.

The liquor-filled man is full of frivolity, profanity, and riotous conduct, and the outpouring of all that an evil spirit inspires. But the Spirit-filled soul is overshadowed, surrounded, and animated by the Holy One Himself. The baptism of the Holy Spirit is the communication of God's life to the nature of man. It is the incoming of God the Spirit to dwell in the soul. It is not synonymous with manifesting the gifts of the Spirit. It is fundamentally different from simply appearing spiritual. It is a purging, cleansing, consuming, energizing presence as of fire.

"Be filled" is in the *imperative mood.* The need is urgent because the years are few. The realization is obligatory and long overdue. We urge upon sinners the acceptance of the Sin Bearer on account of the brevity of life, the certainty and imminence of the final judgment, and the blessedness of salvation, present and future.

In like manner our Christ expects us to be filled with the Spirit for the same and greater reasons. God is in extremity for men today who, thoughtless of themselves, will desire only to be receivers and channels of the Holy Spirit's power. We need not understand His nature nor the process of filling. All we need to know is the fact of His power and the law of His working, and come into compliance with the conditions.

Nothing less will enable us to live a life of victory and fruit bearing. Thus the full joy of redemption becomes a fact of personal experience. And in the waning days of this last age God will fill men with the Spirit as in the time of the early rain. Both John the Baptist and Elijah—prototypes of the Advent people—were filled with the Spirit.

Remember:

"The Father gave His Spirit without measure to His Son, and we also may partake of its fulness."—*The Great Controversy,* p. 477.

### Received by Personal Act of Faith

"Be filled" is in the *passive voice.* We are not bidden to fill ourselves but to *"be* filled," both by and with the Spirit. There must be a Filler. We are to depend upon Him, and the responsibility rests upon Him. This filling is certain because it is based on the unchangeable word of the living God. By meeting the conditions we shall be filled. Yet the proffered gift is one thing, and the personal appropriation is quite another.

The passive voice indicates the surrendered will, the yielded body, and the emptied heart. These are the great prerequisites. We receive Him by a definite, deliberate, conscious, personal act of faith in surrender. But there is more than mere acquiescence, a passive assent to His incoming. There must be actual and active appropriation. In this sense it is active and positive.

Now, just a question before we proceed: *How shall we know if we are filled with the Spirit?* There is danger in looking for some great stir of the emotions, some special revelation of glory, some unusual, gripping sense of majestic presence. Yet this is not usually the case. True, it was that at Pentecost, when He came for the first time. But thereafter it was not usually a dramatic experience. It has in cases been volcanic, turning the life violently upside down. But this is not necessary or general. Let us distinguish between the essence and the mere accompaniments.

The experience of filling is in no two cases identical. Temperaments count for much. "Filling" is just to have the whole being under the Holy Spirit's management and possession. It is God Himself in the presence and person of the Holy Spirit, entering into the throne room of the believer's being, ruling there with power for perfection of life and service. To be filled with the Spirit it is not necessary to have wonderful feelings, but to have Christ glorified within.

### Distinguished Between Mode and Reality

Perhaps an illustration will be helpful: A river may be filled in two different ways. It may be filled with heavy, torrential rains, amid great noise, turmoil, and commotion. Then there is rush and overflow and violence. But there is another way of filling —from the melted snows, calmly, steadily rising until it is full, without any noise or disturbance or commotion. This way it is gradually and enlargingly filled. The methods differ, but in both cases the stream is full.

Similarly, the voiceless wind is known, not by visible perception, but by its effects. In both the Hebrew and the Greek the word for *spirit* is the same as that for *wind*. This at once includes both gentleness and strength. It may be as the quiet evening zephyr, or it may come in the mighty tempest's power. Yet both are the wind.

Thus with the filling of the Spirit. It may be sudden, or it may come down gradually on the soul. It is true that sometimes the filling in apostolic times was accompanied by miraculous phenomena—earthquake, wind, or fire. Yet many times there was nothing of the kind. We must always distinguish between the mode of operation and the thing itself.

"When the Holy Spirit works the human agent, it does not ask us in what way it shall operate. Often it moves in unexpected ways."—*Testimonies to Ministers,* p. 64.

"The Holy Spirit flatters no man, neither does it work according to the devising of any man. Finite, sinful men are not to work the Holy Spirit. When it shall come as a reprover, through any human agent whom God shall choose, it is man's place to hear and obey its voice."—*Ibid.,* p. 65.

### Faith, Fact, and Feeling

We must not arbitrarily mark out in advance the precise channel. It is so easy to form preconceptions which have no warrant in the Bible. Many are looking for physical feelings—joyous thrills and marvelous spiritual shocks—which, if they do not have, they are disheartened. Really, the filling of the Spirit was not meant to be extraordinary. It is a heritage provided as the normal experience for Christians, daily enabling us to live a holy life and to serve effectually, as well as to meet crises by special enduements. We may not even be able to tell the time of the filling, as in some conversions which come in sacred silence. There need be no ecstatic joy.

Fact, faith, feeling, is God's order. The filling may be unique, but it will probably be common. Barnabas never had the experience of Paul, yet both were filled with the Spirit. The fundamental facts were identical. The method is not important; the basic fact is essential. So filling is based not on feelings but on fact. It comes as the result of quiet faith. Thus we read: "That the blessing of Abraham might come on the Gentiles through Jesus Christ; *that we might receive the promise of the Spirit through faith."* Gal. 3:14.

Just as the offer of forgiveness of sins in 1 John 1:9 is a simple offer on one hand and a simple acceptance of the condition on the other, so in Revelation 3:20 there is likewise a transparently simple offer to enter and abide if any man hears and opens the door of the life. It is our human nature possessed by the divine Spirit. Filling brings a blessed consciousness of Christ. We know Him as never before, and His Lordship becomes a conscious, practical reality. One is quietly pervaded with a consciousness of that Presence which reaches back behind the veil into the unseen realities.

There is a sense of God's sovereign ownership, a vision of unswerving purpose, an intimate consciousness of fellowship with Christ, a deep abhorrence of sin, and a joyous comradeship with the Spirit. There is a resultant difference in life and labor. The evidence of the Spirit's power in the case of Elisha was not ecstatic feelings or special manifestations. But when he too smote the waters, they were divided. The evidence was in service.

### Satan's Two Methods of Hindrance

The devil has two outstanding methods he employs with regard to important truths: First, he seeks to hide the vision as long as he can; second, when this is no longer possible he then applies the principle of patronage and distortion. He will take a truth, if he can, out of its true setting, and wrest it into a deadly error. Take, for example, the truth of justification by faith. Through the long weary centuries of the Middle Ages he kept it out of sight until it was forced into view by Luther. Then the devil indirectly adopted it, and adapted and misapplied it until he produced antinomianism, received with ruinous effect by multitudes.

Thus also with the truth of the Holy Spirit. Obscured through the centuries, there came at last a revival of deep interest and investigation of the question of the Holy Spirit within a generation. More books, pamphlets, and tracts have been written on this subject within the last fifty years than in all the time since the invention of printing. It cannot be restrained, so the devil is determined to cast odium on the whole question by bringing the subject into ill repute by the extremes of Pentecostalism, the fanaticism and irrationalities of Holy Roller groups, or the vagaries of mysticism, which discount the historic and minimize dependence upon the Word.

But the devil must not be permitted to rob us of God's truth or to keep from us His provided blessing. We must not be deceived by his cunning plan, and led to discarding Heaven's boon. Our deepest, highest, most urgent need of all needs today is the Holy Spirit, the power and provision of His filling. And the provision we are studying is in violent contrast to all modern perversions and counterfeits. It is most improbable that the staid, rational Adventist people would ever be deceived into the wild vagaries of the cults. Our peril is that we may be tricked into the devil's conspiracy of silence, either through noninvestigation of the true or through disgust engendered by extremes of the false. Note this:

"Great reproach has been cast upon the work of the Holy Spirit, by the errors of a class that, claiming its enlightenment, profess to have no further need of guidance from the word of God. They are governed by impressions which they regard as the voice of God in the soul. But the spirit that controls them is not the Spirit of God. The following of impressions, to the neglect of the Scriptures, can lead only to confusion, to deception and ruin. It serves only to further the designs of the evil one."—Mrs. E. G. White in *Australian Signs of the Times,* July 24, 1911.

"Since the ministry of the Holy Spirit is of vital importance to the church of Christ, it is one of the devices of Satan, through the errors of extremists and fanatics, to cast contempt upon the work of the Spirit, and cause the people of God to neglect this source of strength which our Lord Himself has provided."—*Ibid.*

## Under the Sway of the Spirit

The Holy Spirit, who is to fill us, is not some vague influence or mystic force. He is a divine Person, to be received with deep humility, veneration, and obedience. Therefore it is not a question of our having more of Him, but of His having more of us—yes, all there is of us. So we are seeking not some impersonal power but a fuller knowledge of a Person, greater allegiance to a Person, stronger love for a person, and the absolute sway in the life, of a Person—the Holy Spirit of God.

The Holy Spirit comes to administer in us the rule of Christ. To permit this possession is prerequisite to experiencing His power. But *we* never exercise it; the Holy Spirit always does that. So we are not simply filled with an influence, or a sensation, or a set of ideas, or a mere blessing, *but with a blessed Person.*

We are to do nothing to displease or displace this heavenly Being. We are to treat Him as a welcome Guest, for He is especially sensitive to the reception given Him; never intruding, but gladly entering through the open door and following up every invitation. But He does not come in, or stay in, without our full consent.

Through ages past the Spirit worked according to His sovereign will upon the objects of His grace, visiting solitary hearts at His pleasure. But God has in this dispensation ordained certain universal laws of *His operation* and *our cooperation*. And He Himself most scrupulously recognizes His own laws. He respects the freedom of the human will, never forcing the inestimable blessing of His presence upon unwilling hearts. But He knocks, waiting to be recognized and claimed, working in the soul as we cooperate in obedience.

### Supreme Mystery of God's Grace

The mystery of Bethlehem is incomprehensible, yet it is a positive fact. That a body should be formed for the Son of God by the overshadowing power of the Holy Spirit, and that the Holy Spirit should dwell in Christ of Bethlehem, is indeed a miracle of divine power. But that the same Spirit now comes and dwells in the bodies of sinful men and women is the supreme mystery of God's grace.

The Spirit of God seeks a dwelling place in these bodies of ours. God created sinless man originally for this. Through sin God's primal plan was frustrated, and instead of being full of the Spirit of God, man is full of self and the world. By Adam's first sin the communion was broken and the union ruptured.

But even throughout the reign of sin God is striving to regain possession of the citadel of the soul.

That was the purpose of the coming of the last Adam—to purchase back the lost dominion and to cause man to be again "the temple of the Holy Ghost" (1 Cor. 6:19, 20), thus to restore the broken fellowship between God and man.

Notice:

"From eternal ages it was God's purpose that every created being, from the bright and holy seraph to man, should be a temple for the indwelling of the Creator. Because of sin, humanity ceased to be a temple for God. Darkened and defiled by evil, the heart of man no longer revealed the glory of the divine One. But by the incarnation of the Son of God, the purpose of Heaven is fulfilled. God dwells in humanity, and through saving grace the heart of man becomes again His temple."—*The Desire of Ages,* p. 161.

At creation God made man of the dust of the ground, which was the material basis of the formation. Then He breathed into him the breath of life. Thus man became a spiritual being. Through this inbreathing by God the conscious side of man's nature was born, and thus he was fitted to enter into companionship with God. It has been truly said that it is this that makes man man and differentiates him from the animal world. No lower form of life knows God. Man only was created to look into God's face and know, love, trust, and serve Him. The wisdom to exercise dominion over the lower creation came from God.

Man originally understood and obeyed His laws. And all this came through the Spirit of God that was the agent in the making of man. "The spirit of God hath made me, and the breath of the Almighty hath given me life." Job 33:4. Thus the whole well-being of man was conditioned upon the energy and wisdom of the Spirit. But man lost this. Through resistance he was largely separated from the Holy Spirit.

### Jesus Our Pattern and Exemplar

This principle of life becomes apparent as we study the life of Christ, the Second Man, the last Adam. The relation between the Holy Spirit and the Perfect Man is most illuminating. Every action of body and relation of mind was due to the Holy Spirit. Thus Jesus was our pattern and exemplar in His relation to the Holy Spirit.

His birth, growth, testing, ministry, miracles, death, resurrection, and organization of the church were all through the movings of the Holy Spirit. It was this complete filling and possession by the Spirit that made our Lord what He was as a man. Every action of body and relation of mind was due to the Holy Spirit, as the following scriptures, selected from many of like import, indicate. Note their sweep:

"The angel answered and said unto her, The Holy

Ghost shall come upon thee, and the power of the Highest shall overshadow thee: therefore also that holy thing which shall be born of thee shall be called the Son of God." Luke 1:35.

"Jesus being *full of the Holy Ghost* returned from Jordan, and was led by the Spirit into the wilderness, being forty days tempted of the devil." Luke 4:1, 2.

"Jesus returned *in the power of the Spirit* into Galilee: and there went out a fame of Him through all the region round about." Verse 14.

"How God *anointed Jesus of Nazareth with the Holy Ghost* and with power: who went about doing good, and healing all that were oppressed of the devil; for God was with Him." Acts 10:38.

"If I *cast out devils by the Spirit of God,* then the kingdom of God is come unto you." Matt. 12:28.

"How much more shall the blood of Christ, who *through the eternal Spirit offered Himself* without spot to God, purge your conscience from dead works to serve the living God?" Heb. 9:14.

"Christ also hath once suffered for sins, the just for the unjust, that He might bring us to God, being put to death in the flesh, but *quickened by the Spirit.*" 1 Peter 3:18.

"The former treatise have I made, O Theophilus, of all that Jesus began both to do and teach, until the day in which He was taken up, after that He *through the Holy Ghost* had given commandments unto the apostles whom He had chosen." Acts 1:1, 2.

### Christ's Own Life Spirit-filled

During Christ's childhood and youth He was perpetually under the teaching, molding influence of the Divine Spirit. But at His baptism He entered into a new epoch, a fuller relationship. It was His personal Pentecost. He was endued, anointed, without measure. (John 3:34.) He was full of the Holy Spirit. He was conscious that the Spirit of the Lord had come upon Him, anointing Him to preach. His miracles and words were under that inspiration. Through the eternal Spirit He offered Himself on the cross, and upon His resurrection by the Holy Spirit (1 Peter 3:18), He was "declared to be the Son of God with power." Rom. 1:4.

Every grace of Christ's character is directly attributable to the Holy Spirit. The universality and indispensability of the Spirit's work for man is indicated by His names, which follow: He is the Spirit of life (Rom. 8:2), Spirit of adoption (Rom. 8:15), Spirit of truth (John 14:17), Spirit of wisdom (Eph. 1:17), Spirit of power and of love (2 Tim. 1:7), Spirit of faith (2 Cor. 4:13), Spirit of grace (Heb. 10:29), and Spirit of glory (1 Peter 4:14). And the characteristic constantly emphasized is *Holy* Spirit.

Jesus was "full" of the Holy Spirit. And the same Spirit who lived in the body of Jesus, who wept through His tears and loved in His sacrifices, wants to dwell in us as the very presence of our dear Redeemer.

## Occasional in Old Testament Times

Through sin man has distanced himself from God. Sin is something unnatural that has poisoned every succeeding generation. The work of Jesus was to deliver from this sin element, and change the unnatural back to the spiritual. In Old Testament times the Spirit's ministry for man was partial, and only occasional in its fullness. Special men were filled for the accomplishment of a special work. Thus Joseph, Gideon, and others were filled with the Spirit.

When we reach the approaching incarnation of Christ, John, His forerunner, was filled with the Holy Spirit from his birth (Luke 1:15); Elisabeth was filled for her salutation (Luke 1:41); and Zacharias was filled for uttering his prophecy (Luke 1:67-69).

"From the beginning God has been working by His Holy Spirit through human instrumentalities for the accomplishment of His purpose in behalf of the fallen race. This was manifest in the lives of the patriarchs. To the church in the wilderness also, in the time of Moses, God gave His 'good Spirit to instruct them.' And in the days of the apostles He wrought mightily for His church through the agency of the Holy Spirit. The same power that sustained the patriarchs, that gave Caleb and Joshua faith and courage, and that made the work of the apostolic church effective, has upheld God's faithful children in every succeeding age. It was through the power of the Holy Spirit that during the Dark Ages the Waldensian Christians helped to prepare the way for the Reformation. It was the same power that made successful the efforts of the noble men and women who pioneered the way for the establishment of modern missions, and for the translation of the Bible into the languages and dialects of all nations and peoples." —*Acts of the Apostles,* p. 53.

## Not Simply for Privileged Few

To be filled is to be under the guidance, dominance, power, and control of the Spirit. But there is a clear line of demarcation between the new and the old dispensation. Being "filled with the Spirit" is no longer reserved for the privileged few. It has now been put within the reach of all. So Peter declared in his Pentecostal sermon. (Acts 2:17, 18.)

At Pentecost *all* the one hundred and twenty apostles and disciples, men and women, were "filled" with the Holy Spirit. (Acts 2:4.) Again, in Acts 4:31 we read, "When they had prayed, the place was shaken where they were assembled together; and they were *all* filled with the Holy Ghost, and they spake the word of God with boldness." New converts were filled. Peter was again filled (Acts 4:8); Stephen and the other six deacons were filled (Acts 6:3-5; 7:55); Barnabas was filled (Acts 11:22-24); Paul was filled (Acts 13:9, 10).

The words *filled* and *full* occur again and again in the book of Acts, and in three forms of the verb—

*filled, being filled,* and *full.* Christians were filled as there was need. It was their normal condition, especially when the need was greatest. The believers were taught to expect it. Not to be filled was the exception rather than the rule in apostolic times, hence Paul's inquiry at Ephesus.

### No Monopoly on the Holy Spirit

It will be observed that there is no formal conclusion to the book of Acts. God desired it to be prolonged throughout the centuries of this dispensation of the Spirit. It is not simply for the sickly and saintly in appearance. The apostolic experience was given as a specimen and a type. God wants *us* to be filled. He asks, Are you willing?

Our text in Ephesians 5:18 implies that all Christian believers *may* be filled with the Spirit. Some people would almost seem to believe that a few people have the monopoly on the Holy Spirit. The truth is the precise opposite, that *the Holy Spirit has the monopoly of only a few people.* The Holy Spirit is promised, and God will give the Spirit in answer to prayer. "If ye then, being evil, know how to give good gifts unto your children: how much more shall your heavenly Father give the Holy Spirit to them that ask Him?" Luke 11:13. Until Christ gave this admonition and promise, the thought of asking for the Spirit was largely foreign to the economy of the past.

‹‹‹-‹‹‹-‹‹‹-‹‹‹-‹‹‹

# CHAPTER ELEVEN

# After Rebirth Comes Infilling

THE distinction between the Spirit's work in *regeneration* and in our being *filled with the Spirit* should be clearly defined and understood. Through regeneration by the Spirit (John 3:5, 8), men dead in sin are made alive. Libertines sunken in beastliness, blasphemers who have spoken against God, and infidels who have published their shame to the world, are born again by the Spirit. Into everyone so born, the Spirit enters, imparting spiritual life: "If any man have not the Spirit of Christ, he is none of His." Rom. 8:9.

This is a great step in the experience of a human life. But this is not necessarily synonymous with the "filling" of the Spirit. It is one thing to receive the Spirit, but quite another to receive His power and fullness. There is a vast difference between *having* the Holy Spirit, and *being filled* with the Holy Spirit. They could and should come together, but often they do not. The difference is in degree. Egypt has the Nile the year round, but its fertilizing, fructifying power is practically dormant until it is in flood and overflows its banks with its burden of enriching silt. Then it bestows its needed blessings upon every foot of land it touches.

### Christ's Lordship Follows His Saviourship

If you are a twice-born person, you have the Holy Spirit in you; but does He *fill* you? That is the crucial question. Many believe in Jesus, yet never get beyond the first stage. But there must be an experience beyond the new birth. And that is this filling by and with the Comforter. Through the new birth one passes from death to life; through being filled, one becomes a partaker of the fuller life.

It is a relationship into which we may or may not enter, though we are exhorted, yea, divinely commanded to, in Ephesians 5; and in order to abide through the time when there will be no high priestly intercession, when mercy ceases and forgiveness for transgressions is ended, we must enter. (Zeph. 2:3.) Unless we are filled, this Gift of all gifts, this heavenly Guest, this mighty, holy Being, is relegated to some obscure corner of the heart, and is excluded from other parts of the life.

Oh, let us make Him the welcome guest, to whom every part of the being is thrown wide open! Let the Holy Spirit have every nook and corner of His purchased temple. Life in this relationship is the greatest privilege of the Christian.

Thus we see that the Lordship of Jesus is often distinct from His Saviourship. At Pentecost the Holy Spirit settled not only upon but in the disciples. (John 14:16, 17.) He took up His dwelling in their individual lives, making them His own possession.

He made them His seat, or "holy see," His permanent abiding place.

As in frontier days the pioneers took up squatters' claims, so the Holy Spirit took up His claim in the disciples. He entered the territory of their lives, that He would not otherwise possess, for the devil had robbed God of His dominion in man. But now the Holy Spirit took possession and proceeded to dwell in them. Through all ages He has striven *with* men; in the old dispensation He generally came *upon* men, fitting them for special service; now He desires to dwell *in* them. In olden times He dwelt in the prophets (1 Peter 1:11); now He desires to dwell in all believers (2 Cor. 6:16).

### Filled to Measure of Capacity

This was the great aim of Jesus. After He had trained and educated the disciples for three years, He merely led them to the point of waiting for the promise of the Father. And what Jesus has promised we may obtain. This was the object of Peter's sermon at Pentecost. After men had been pricked in their hearts, Peter said, "Repent, and be baptized every one of you in the name of Jesus Christ for the remission of sins, and *ye shall receive the gift of the Holy Ghost.*" Acts 2:38. This was the purpose of Paul when he asked the question and wrote the admonition to the Ephesians. (Acts 19:2; Eph. 5:18.)

There is no true worship, personal victory, or

effective service except through the indwelling and increasing operation of the Holy Spirit. Although the disciples were filled at Pentecost, they no doubt had much more to receive, but each was filled up to the measure of his capacity. You can stand on the deck of a ship in mid-ocean and see the mighty sun reflected in the depths; or you can see the same sun in a tiny pool in the back yard or in the dewdrop of the morning. The sun has a way of accommodating itself to its reflectors. So God can fill any man, whatever his capacity, if he will only let Him.

If the sun can fill a flower with all its light in many tints and colors; if the cloud can drink in his brightsome rays until they glow with glorious tints, surely the Holy Spirit can cause His light of holiness to shine forth in human lives. And this consciousness and indwelling of the Holy Spirit in man is the most wonderful thing that can come into a human experience.

Let us not go half the way or be two thirds filled. Our witness is in proportion to the fullness of His indwelling. Let us open the whole life for God to fill. We must be filled just as the air fills our lungs and the blood our arteries and veins. The Greek word usually translated "to fill" is *"pleroein,"* to fill full, so full that there is no room left.

The expression "filled" suggests the idea of a vessel with capacity to receive and contain. God is the potter; man is the vessel. David speaks of the cup and Paul of the earthen vessel. Yes, man is a vessel designed to receive the Spirit of God—a vessel enlarged in proportion as it is filled and refilled.

### Emptied Before Being Filled

A once-for-all filling is not taught in the Bible. There are fresh needs and supplies imparted only by God; each additional bestowment comes from above. Pentecost was the beginning, but the disciples were filled again and again, repeatedly. Peter needed refillings. So while the initial infilling is an important crisis, it is to be followed by fresh communications. Whenever a new emergency arose, the early disciples sought a refilling.

True, there was a habitual fullness, but there were occasional fuller experiences for special purposes. They could even be full without implying fullness to the utmost, for those special times. Titus speaks of the "renewing of the Holy Ghost" (Titus 3:5); and Peter of "times of refreshing" (Acts 3:19). The trouble is that many are trying to do God's work with the power they received ten years ago. We are all leaky vessels. We have to keep under the fountain perpetually to keep full.

To be filled involves first, being emptied. Self and sin are thus displaced. It is the operation of the law of exclusion. There is room for various things in a tumbler. But if filled with water, there is no room for the air that had previously filled it. Two diverse things cannot at one and the same time occupy the same place. Self and the Holy Spirit cannot occupy the same heart throne. I cannot still be something, and God be everything. *And self can never cast out self.* Don't attempt to make room. Simply yield, and "the Lord will come suddenly to His temple." In each heart there is a cross and a throne. If Jesus is on the throne, self is on the cross.

"As you empty the heart of self, you must accept the righteousness of Christ. . . . If you open the door of the heart, Jesus will supply the vacuum by the gift of His Spirit."—Mrs. E. G. White in *Review and Herald,* Feb. 23, 1892.

We must be emptied. Wind always blows toward a vacuum. In the "upper chamber" before Pentecost the disciples were being emptied, and a vacuum was made. The son of thunder was emptied of his thunder, that he might be filled with love. Doubting Thomas was emptied of his doubt, that he might be filled with faith. Presumptuous Peter was emptied of his presumption and fickleness, that he might be filled with the power and steadfastness of God. Then came the sound of the mighty rushing wind that announced the advent of the Spirit that filled them.

How good God is to give to man this gift supreme! History tells of a king who wished to express affection for a private soldier. So he gave him his own richly jeweled cup. "This is too great a gift for me to receive," the soldier said. "But it is not too great for me to give," was the king's generous reply. So we might say of the Holy Spirit.

### Indispensable for Completing Our Task

Having progressed thus far in these studies, the question has surely formed in our minds: *Is the promised Spirit imperative for us?* Is He the indispensable necessity for the completion of our twofold task—to make ready a people prepared for the Lord, and to finish the final work of warning and entreaty for the world? The responsive question is inescapable: How else can it be done? We have more to fight against than had the early church. There are a thousand things to keep a man away from God.

The world is friendly to the church today, and its temptations are consequently more subtle and dangerous. Its smile is more bland and alluring. The gulf has been narrowed between the two. Rationalism in the popular churches has robbed the world of simple faith in God, so that we now have to breast the current of modernism. This secularizing spirit of the day has even leavened our own ranks, and many are perceptibly or imperceptibly losing out. We read:

"The Spirit of God is departing from many among His people. Many have entered into dark, secret paths, and some will never return. They will continue to stumble to their ruin."—*Testimonies to Ministers,* p. 90.

The multiplying of means and endeavors will not turn the tide. The inward, invisible *power* of sin can be met only by the inward, invisible *power* of Christ through the Holy Spirit. When He fills the heart He quenches our temptations as the sparks that fall into the ocean are extinguished. We need His life as the basis for living our own new life. (Gal. 2:20.) We need Him for the development of Christian character with its love, joy, peace, long-suffering, gentleness, goodness, faith, meekness, and self-control; for these are His graces, not ours.

For the development of these fruits we need the pressure of the divine sap in the branches. "The love of God hath been shed abroad in our hearts *through the Holy Spirit which was given unto us.*" Rom. 5:5, A.R.V. We need Him for spiritual enlightenment. "Ye have an unction from the Holy One, and ye know all things." 1 John 2:20. We need Him as the secret token, the necessary assurance, of our sonship. "The Spirit Himself beareth witness with our spirit, that we are children of God." Rom. 8:16, A.R.V. "Hereby know we that we dwell in Him, and He in us, because He hath given us of His Spirit." 1 John 4:13.

## Mighty Undercurrent of the Spirit

We need Him for steadfastness in this age of bewilderment and confusion, when storms and cross currents sweep over the surface. We must not be like the canal I saw at Memramcook, New Brunswick.

From the window of the little French hotel I watched the daily phenomenon of a stream flowing both ways. Normally it flowed down toward the bay, but when the terrific rise of tide came in from the Bay of Fundy, it absolutely reversed the current, so that it flowed the other way under the pressure of the tide. Just so it is with multitudes today carried hither and yon by the current. But this need not be.

Often an iceberg in its journey southward in the Atlantic will encounter the Gulf Stream, which flows north. But because the larger portion of the ice is below the surface, it reaches down to another larger stream, which is the return current, and it proceeds steadily on its way southward.

So the soul may be so fully immersed, as it were, in the mighty undercurrent of the Holy Spirit that in spite of surface streams we shall find the great undercurrent of His holy life powerful enough to keep the set of the soul Godward. Though it is the "blood of Jesus Christ that *cleanseth* us from all sin," it is the Holy Spirit of God that *empowers* us against sin and for service.

Yes, truly we need Him for power in service, that it may be acceptably performed, His fullness never comes merely to make us happy or holy. Power is coupled with willingness to witness. It is given to be used for service not for self. We need His convicting cooperation that the Word, which is a "fire," may burn in the souls of men, that as a "hammer" it may break sin-hardened hearts, and that as a "sword" it may cut its way through sin and unbelief.

We are *born again* primarily for our own needs, but He *fills* us for service. As soon as Jesus was baptized "with the Holy Ghost, and with fire," He went about doing good. As soon as the disciples were filled, they "began to speak," and the era of mission endeavor began. The vessel is filled, not for its own sake, but for the Master's use.

### Purposes and Results of Filling

Note the purposes for which men were filled in apostolic times: for witness (Acts 2:4), for answering objections (Acts 4:8), for speaking boldly God's word (Acts 4:31), for serving tables (Acts 6:2, 3), for suffering persecution and martyrdom (Acts 7:55), for exposing evil (Acts 13:9, 10), for praising or giving thanks (Eph. 5:18-20). Surely these various operations of the Spirit were all intensely practical. Now note:

"As a people, we are not doing one fiftieth of what we might do as active missionaries. If we were only vitalized by the Holy Spirit, there would be a hundred missionaries where there is now one."—*Counsels on Health,* p. 507.

"The number of workers in the ministry is not to be lessened, but greatly increased. Where there is now one minister in the field, twenty are to be added; and if the Spirit of God controls them, these twenty will so present the truth that twenty more will be added."—*Gospel Workers,* pp. 65, 66.

Glance next at Paul's picture of the results of being filled with the Spirit. The rest of the epistle to the Ephesians, after the admonition to "be filled" in chapter 5:18, might be cataloged by verses as follows:

1. (Verse 19) Songs in the heart—holy joy thus finding vent.

2. (Verse 20) Spirit of thanksgiving—recognition that God has taken charge, and all adverse conditions are of His choosing or permission, all things working together for good to them who are called.

3. (Verse 21) Self-subjugation—nothing but the Holy Spirit can bring this about.

4. (Eph. 5:22-33; 6:1-5) Applied in daily life:
   a. Wives (Eph. 5:22).
   b. Husbands (verse 22).
   c. Children (Eph. 6:1).
   d. Fathers (verse 4).
   e. Servants (verse 5).

5. (Verse 10) Finally, strength with power.
   a. The whole armor (verses 11-17).
   b. Prayer and intercession (verse 18).
   c. Boldness of utterance (verse 19).

# CHAPTER TWELVE

ᘓᘓᘓᘓᘓᘓᘓᘓᘓᘓᘓ

# The Fruitage of the Infilling

THERE are three outstanding things that the fullness of the Spirit brings: The *presence* of Christ; the *likeness* of Christ; and the *power* of Christ. Let us amplify briefly:

First, the filling of the Holy Spirit brings *a new and vivid consciousness of Jesus' presence.* Before, He is indistinct, the glimpses of His face are few and far between, and the moments of true communion fitful. In the days of His earthly sojourn Jesus' presence was everything. He met every trouble and supplied every need. In storm He quieted the waters. When the multitudes were hungry He supplied food. But everything depended upon having Him with them. His presence was their help. So also now all depends upon His presence with us.

## Gives Strength and Confidence

It is this consciousness and provision that gives strength and confidence. By the Holy Spirit, Jesus takes up His abode in us as an Abiding Presence. That is what we need. It is accomplished only by this filling. "That He would grant you, according to the riches of His glory, to be strengthened with might by His Spirit in the inner man; that Christ may dwell in your hearts by faith." Eph. 3:16, 17. So we find expressed in modern times:

"In the plan of restoring in men the divine image, it was provided that the Holy Spirit should move upon human minds, and be as the presence of Christ, a molding agency upon human character."—*Review and Herald,* Feb. 12, 1895, p. 97.

"The impartation of the Spirit was the impartation of the very life of Christ."—*Ibid.,* June 13, 1899, p. 369.

"Before this the Spirit had been in the world; from the very beginning of the work of redemption He had been moving upon men's hearts. But while Christ was on earth, the disciples had desired no other helper. Not until they were deprived of His presence would they feel the need of the Spirit, and then He would come."

"The Holy Spirit is Christ's representative, but divested of the personality of humanity, and independent thereof."—*Ibid.,* Nov. 19, 1908, p. 15.

"The Holy Spirit is the vital presence of God."—*Signs of the Times,* Aug. 7, 1901, p. 2.

Again we are told:

"The work of the Holy Spirit is immeasurably great. It is from this source that power and efficiency come to the worker for God; and the Holy Spirit is the Comforter, as the personal presence of Christ to the soul. He who looks to Christ in simple, childlike faith, is made a partaker of the divine nature through the agency of the Holy Spirit."—MRS. E. G. WHITE in *Review and Herald,* Nov. 29, 1892.

It is this personal fellowship with Jesus that makes the difference between the new life and the old. We are invited to give ourselves up to a life of unbroken communion with Jesus. May our hearts fully respond to this. The union between us and Jesus is not a union of flesh with flesh, but of Spirit with spirit. "Now the Lord is the Spirit" (2 Cor. 3:17, A.R.V.); and "he that is joined unto the Lord is one spirit." 1 Cor. 6:17.

The Christ we need today is the living, reigning, present, working Christ, His Spirit witnessing with our spirit, His Spirit taking possession of and ruling our spirit, His Spirit revealing His life, power, and obedience in our lives, transforming and making us *real* Christians, yet without interfering with our individuality or destroying our personality. Listen:

"If we consent, He will so identify Himself with our thoughts and aims, so blend our hearts and minds into conformity to His will, that when obeying Him we shall be but carrying out our own impulses."— *The Desire of Ages,* p. 668.

### Brings the Likeness of Jesus

Second, the filling brings the *likeness of Jesus.* When we sense His presence, there will be revealed an amount of sin and self, flesh and failure, that will amaze us. The disciples had Jesus' external presence with them during His fleshly sojourn, but did not exhibit His likeness, which comes only through His indwelling. He was humble; they were proud. He was unselfish; they were selfish. But when the Holy Spirit filled them, He brought the characteristics, the disposition, the very likeness of Jesus within. *This is reproduction, not imitation.* The empty places of our lives will be filled with His fullness, as the tide of the sea fills the hollows of the shore. Read it:

"What was the result of the outpouring of the Spirit upon the day of Pentecost?—The glad tidings of a risen Saviour were carried to the utmost bounds of the inhabited world. The hearts of the disciples were surcharged with a benevolence so full, so deep, so far-reaching, that it impelled them to go to the ends of the earth, testifying, 'God forbid that I should glory, save in the cross of our Lord Jesus Christ.' Gal. 6:14.

"As they proclaimed the truth as it is in Jesus, hearts yielded to the power of the message. The church beheld converts flocking to her from all directions. Backsliders were reconverted. Sinners united with Christians in seeking the pearl of great price. Those who had been the bitterest opponents of the gospel became its champions. The prophecy was fulfilled, The weak shall be 'as David,' and the house of David 'as the angel of the Lord.' Every Christian saw in his brother the divine similitude of love and benevolence. One interest prevailed. One subject of emulation swallowed up all others. The only ambition of the believers was to reveal the likeness of Christ's character and to labor for the enlargement of His kingdom."—*Testimonies,* vol. 8, pp. 19, 20.

### Brings the Power of Jesus

Third, the filling brings *the power of Jesus.* We all want power, and have so little of it. Our supreme need is power. This truism is so familiar as to be commonplace, but so important as to need to be repeated until the church is awakened. Power belongeth unto God, but He has given it unto us in Christ through the Holy Spirit. God does not give it to me to have of myself; but when He fills me He exercises His power in me. (Col. 1:29.)

"We need the Pentecostal energy. This will come; for the Lord has promised to send His Spirit as the all-conquering power."—*Gospel Workers,* p. 308.

In the light of these mighty facts can there be any question but that the filling of the Holy Spirit is our greatest individual and collective need today?

"God can teach you more in one moment by His Holy Spirit than you could learn from the great men of the earth."—*Testimonies to Ministers,* p. 119.

"The presence of the Spirit with God's workers will give the proclamation of truth a power that not all the honor or glory of the world could give."—*Acts of the Apostles,* p. 51.

God grant that wondrous infilling!

### Abandonment and Abiding Requisite

What, then, are the conditions of receiving this needed filling? It is provided and offered to all, yet comparatively few receive it. Many pray for it, yet without result. Why? Ah, because they are unwilling to pay the price. And what is the price? It is the fulfillment of the conditions upon which the filling is contingent and the power is operative. We have not, because we do not meet the conditions.

"In the great and measureless gift of the Holy Spirit are contained all of heaven's resources. It is not because of any restriction on the part of God that the riches of His grace do not flow earthward to men. If all were willing to receive, all would become filled with His Spirit."—*Christ's Object Lessons,* p. 419.

We are also told:

"Christ has promised the gift of the Holy Spirit to His church, and the promise belongs to us as much as to the first disciples. *But like every other promise, it is given on conditions.* There are many who believe and profess to claim the Lord's promise; they talk *about* Christ and *about* the Holy Spirit, yet receive no benefit. They do not surrender the soul to be guided and controlled by the divine agencies. We cannot use the Holy Spirit. The Spirit is to use us. Through the Spirit God works in His people to 'will and to do of His good pleasure.' But many will not submit to this. They want to manage themselves. This is why they do not receive the heavenly gift. Only to those who wait humbly upon God, who watch for His guidance and grace, is the Spirit given. The power of God awaits their demand and reception. This promised blessing, claimed by faith, brings all other blessings in its train. It is given according to the riches of the grace of Christ, *and He is ready to supply every soul according to the capacity to receive."—The Desire of Ages,* p. 672.

In general, these conditions are *abandonment* and *abiding,* the initial and the continuous conditions. There must be purity of motive, full and gladsome surrender, and implicit, present trust. We must realize and acknowledge our lack. The first requisite to treatment and recovery from a disease is the knowledge that one is sick. We must realize the filling is *for the last generation as well as for the apostolic generation.* We must reach the place where we feel we must have it at any cost, where every faculty of the nature, and every moment of the life shall be His to fill, with no more independent control—a vessel emptied, to be completely filled.

There is no enduement apart from thirsting. "I will pour water upon him that is thirsty, . . . My Spirit upon thy seed." Isa. 44:3. There is no enduement apart from or except for obedience; it is "to them that obey." Acts 5:32. It is not bestowed apart from prayer. "When they had prayed, the place was shaken . . . ; and they were all filled with the Holy Ghost."

Acts 4:31. The first disciples received the Spirit on
their knees. Let us get down before God. And let us
not be in a hurry to get up. Nor is the Holy Spirit
received apart from faith. "That we might receive the
promise of the Spirit through faith." Gal. 3:14. Let
us ask in faith believing. "Ask ye of the Lord rain in
the time of the latter rain; so the Lord shall make
bright clouds, and give them showers of rain, to every
one grass in the field." Zech. 10:1.

### What Do We Want With the Spirit?

Amplifying again, there is first of all *intense, unselfish desire.* What do I want with the Holy Spirit?
It is a searching interrogation. Do I want Him solely
to glorify Jesus? James and John were never filled
until they answered that question. Paul was filled only
because to him to live was Christ. (Phil. 1:21.)
Peter was never filled until he was ready to say, "Why
look ye so earnestly on us, as though by our own
power or holiness we had made this man to walk?"
Acts 3:12.

God searches hearts and sifts motives. The fullness of the Holy Spirit will never be given to gratify
ambition or to make us famous for saintliness or in
service. Such is a misuse of a rightful thing. If the
object for which it is sought is vanity or self-aggran-
dizement, the fulfillment is impossible. He who
desires it for the sake of being great, will no more
have it than Simon Magus, who sought to purchase it.

Is it for self or Christ? In other words, *Do I want the Holy Spirit for the same reason that He wants Me?* For we must receive the Holy Spirit Himself when we receive His power; they are inseparable. It must be God's will, nothing less, nothing more, nothing else.

Second, there must be *emptiness*—a definite, conscious surrender for Him to have His rightful place in me. It is wholehearted, positive yieldedness, unquestioned abandonment, and positive, final, irrevocable consecration. It is full committal of the whole life, without reservation, for salvation, sanctification, and service. God can occupy only as much as we yield.

This is the only way to get, and the only way to keep, filled. As in 2 Kings 3:16, 17, we are to "make this valley full of ditches" to be filled. Instead of praying for God to give us something more, we must give Him something more. The question is, Am I willing to be small enough and weak enough so that Christ can be all in all? This will separate us from the world quicker than anything else. It will automatically solve many a problem.

### Yield All Hindering Obstacles

Nor will God answer while our personal life is wrong. We shall not be filled unless we are in harmony with both God and man. The spirit of rivalry, hatred, disgust, or dislike will certainly prevent the fulfillment, and constant prayer for the person involved is the supreme antidote for hates. Jealousy or gossiping about others, criticizing or spreading evil reports, the exaggeration of little slips, or the imputing of wrong motives, becoming judges of evil thoughts—these are the hindrances that are so often fatal.

"When we bring our hearts into unity with Christ, and our lives into harmony with His work, the Spirit that fell on the disciples on the day of Pentecost will fall on us."—*Testimonies,* vol. 8, p. 246.

Third, comes *obedience.* The promise rests upon simple obedience. *And only the obedient remnant have the right to ask and expect to be filled.* It was after thirty years of implicit obedience that Jesus came to be baptized and said, "Thus it becometh us to fulfil all righteousness." Matt. 3:15. Then He was baptized with the Spirit. And He went on with His obedience until He reached the limit of fidelity on the cross, where He was "obedient unto death, even the death of the cross." Phil. 2:8. And it was this obedience that secured for us the best blessing that heaven has to bestow, which brings all other blessings in its train.

When Israel made a tabernacle for the Holy One to dwell among them, Moses and the people built everything exactly "as the Lord commanded." Eighteen times in the last two chapters of Exodus this expression occurs. Then the tabernacle was filled with the glory of God (Ex. 40:34), for it was a structure built according to His expressed will. And thereafter its service was directed by the divine Presence. The same was true as regards Solomon's Temple. (2 Chron. 5:13, 14.) So God will make His home today only in the human heart where there is a willingness for God's will to be done.

The "cloud of Jehovah" was upon the tabernacle by day and the fire by night in the sight of all Israel in all their journeys. (Ex. 40:38.) And Numbers 9:15-23 tells how Israel was divinely guided. Yet they never knew a day ahead where or when they were to go, but were under the direct control and regulation of the Presence in the cloud.

### Appropriate the Gift by Faith

The fourth and last condition is *faith to believe that God accepts my surrender and bestows the blessing.* It involves appropriating by faith the promise. Faith involves a conviction that God's Word is true, and that His promises are sure. The emptying is largely negative, while faith is positive. It is simply appropriating what God has offered when the conditions are met. It is reckoning that God has done His part. It is not waiting for some sensation but daring to believe God first. Then God supplies the fact. And it becomes an experience more and more real. Receiving is simply faith in action.

There is a sharp difference between appropriating

the blessing and experiencing it. Many become discouraged because they do not at once experience the feeling of enjoyment expected. In seeking forgiveness of sin, many want to feel first and trust afterward. But this is a reversal. We must avoid waiting to see special results before trusting. Receiving Christ as Lord through the Holy Spirit is as simple as receiving Him as Saviour. There is no need for emotion. There may be emotion, but it is not necessary.

When in response to the offer of Christ we forsake all, counting it all loss for the filling of the Holy Spirit, then from the moment we really believe, He accepts our surrender and bestows the fullness of the Spirit. When the conditions are met the fulfilling answer is as sure as if we had seen it written in heaven.

So let us receive Him with open, yielding, hungering, thirsting, believing, accepting, absorbing hearts, as the dry sand receives the rain, the empty sponge the moisture, or the vacuum the air. When we put ourselves at His disposal and in faith receive the gift, the Holy Spirit takes possession; the empty vessel is filled. But it must first be empty.

Such are the conditions.

### The Experience of the Disciples

Look for a moment at the experience of the disciples. God did not give the Spirit to the unprepared. Mark the steps:

First, *they forsook all to follow Jesus.* They let
go the world, the possessions and the opinions of
men, the fishing nets, and the seat of custom. Except
we forsake all we cannot be His disciples. Everything
is to be sacrificed and subordinated. But beware if
there be a secret conviction that you have not forsaken
all. Thus there is a certain moral relation to Christ
that is necessary.

Second, *they were brought to utter self-despair.*
For a man must deny *self.* This is a much more difficult task. They were filled with self-confidence at the
last supper. Then came Gethsemane, when they fell
asleep, and the arrest and trial when they fled, and
from a distance witnessed the supreme tragedy of
the ages. They were too ashamed to look each other
in the face. They never knew they were so faithless
and treacherous.

The Sabbath of the tomb was a day of death and
unutterable anguish. It broke down all reliance in
self, all trust in anything earthly. In utter despair
of themselves they turned to Christ. Then on the
resurrection day Jesus breathed on them and said,
"Receive ye the Holy Ghost."

Third, *they accepted by faith the promise of the
Spirit.* During the ten days in waiting and prayer the
devil doubtless tempted them over their unworthiness.
They understood very little of the Old Testament
promises. They believed because Jesus promised it.
And that is what faith is—doing just what Christ

says. They were prepared; and so they were filled.

A word should be added on *how the Holy Spirit is to be retained.* A fire cannot be maintained without fresh fuel. So the fullness of the Holy Spirit is dependent upon abiding in the conditions of the initial receiving—constant, implicit obedience, constant separation unto the divine purpose, constant study of the Word, time in daily secret communion, shunning all impurity (Jude 19), avoiding laziness (2 Tim. 1:6, 7), and willingness for complete identification in a life of service.

### Shipwrecked Because of Self

This is not a state from which we cannot fall, or where we are untempted. Alas, the shipwrecks of men who were once mightily used! Many a bright flame has been snuffed out by an inordinate desire to shine. New privileges bring new responsibilities, and new responsibilities create new perils. Can God trust us? Not unless our motives are pure.

There are three fundamental expressions in this relation that should be noted: Resisting (Acts 7:57) seemingly has to do with the Spirit's regenerative work; grieving (Eph. 4:30) has unquestionably to do with His indwelling or filling; and quenching (1 Thess. 5:19) has to do with enduement for service. The latter term presupposes the presence of fire, and the suggestion carries one back to the fire of Pentecost and the movement inaugurated there.

A boy once had a dove so tame that he would perch on his shoulder and take food from his hand. One day the lad held out a tempting morsel. As the bird came to eat, he closed his hand over the food. The bird turned away disappointed. Again he opened his hand. The second time the bird came, more timidly. And once more the hand was closed. With drooping wings the dove went a short distance away. Yet again the hand was extended. The bird hesitated, then came slowly forward. When he was about to take the food the hand closed for the third time. Then the dove spread his wings and flew away, and the lad never saw him again. Such is the fate of those who at last drive away the Spirit, the heavenly dove.

"After God has shown individuals their sins and given them grace to overcome, and His Spirit has been long striving with them, He will not work a miracle to prevent the sure result of resisting that Spirit and persisting in a wrong course. There is a boundary to His grace and mercy; and when this boundary is passed, the aid of His Spirit, so wickedly refused and insulted, is withdrawn, and the soul is given over to the worst of tyrants,—the power of a perverted will. If we are closely connected with sacred things, and yet do not realize their importance, the heart will become so hard that the most earnest appeals will not move it to contrition."—MRS. E. G. WHITE in *Bible Echo,* June, 1888.

₭₭-₭₭-₭₭-₭₭-₭₭-

# CHAPTER THIRTEEN

# The Challenge to the Remnant

IN THE conclusion of this movement, the Spirit of prophecy says, there will be few great men. God wants us to take our eyes off men, and place our dependence upon the Holy Spirit for the finishing of our work.

Hear it:

"God will work a work in our day that but few anticipate. He will raise up and exalt among us those who are taught rather by the unction of His Spirit, than by the outward training of scientific institutions. These facilities are not to be despised or condemned; they are ordained of God, but they can furnish only the exterior qualifications. God will manifest that He is not dependent on learned, self-important mortals." —*Testimonies*, vol. 5, p. 82.

Oh, what a revolution, what a revival, what a change will come, when God's remnant church is filled with the Holy Spirit! Weakness and fear will be superseded by courage and power. Obviously the cause of our lack is to be sought not in God but in ourselves. And there is a steadily growing realization of need, a developing consciousness of lack. It is a happy omen. God haste the day when our infilling shall be complete!

### Latter-Rain Power Our Need

It is impossible truly to preach a latter-rain gospel save in the power of the latter rain. It is not hard work that breaks us down, it is the toil of working without the requisite power. How we need it! How we should pray for it!

"We are to pray for the impartation of the Spirit as the remedy for sin-sick souls. The church needs to be converted, and why should we not prostrate ourselves at the throne of grace, as representatives of the church, and from a broken heart and contrite spirit make earnest supplication that the Holy Spirit shall be poured out upon us from on high?"—*Testimonies to Ministers,* p. 64.

"My brethren and sisters, plead for the Holy Spirit. God stands back of every promise He has made. With your Bibles in your hands, say: 'I have done as Thou hast said. I present Thy promise, "Ask, and it shall be given you; seek, and ye shall find; knock, and it shall be opened unto you." ' "—*Testimonies,* vol. 8, p. 23.

Notice these further earnest appeals:

"O, how we need the divine presence! For the baptism of the Holy Spirit every worker should be breathing out his prayer to God."—*Testimonies to Ministers,* p. 170.

"Why do we not hunger and thirst for the gift of the Spirit, since this is the means by which we are to receive power? Why do we not talk of it, pray for it, preach concerning it? The Lord is more willing to give the Holy Spirit to us than parents are to give good gifts to their children. For the baptism of the Spirit every worker should be pleading with God."—*Testimonies,* vol. 8, p. 22.

Here is the counsel we need:

"For the daily baptism of the Spirit, every worker should offer his petition to God. Companies of Christian workers should gather to ask for special help, for heavenly wisdom, that they may know how to plan and execute wisely. Especially should they pray that God will baptize His chosen ambassadors in mission fields with a rich measure of His Spirit. The presence of the Spirit with God's workers will give the proclamation of truth a power that not all the honor or glory of the world could give."—*Acts of the Apostles,* pp. 50, 51.

When we want men to fill various important posts, do we seek men "full of the Holy Ghost and of wisdom"? Shall not this be the deciding factor? Here is our lack, our weakness. I am convinced that every candidate for the ministry ought to be asked Paul's question to the Ephesians, "Did ye receive the Holy Spirit when ye believed?" and an intelligent, conscientious answer should be expected.

How can we play like children on the seashore with their buckets and shovels, making little heaps of sand which they call mountains, and little puddles which they call oceans, when the mighty Himalayas of God's power and the fathomless oceans of divine provision await the explorations of faith?

### It Is Not Numbers That Count

The hour is late. We must not delay. Israel spent forty years wandering, when she could have gone straight into the Promised Land in eleven days. Our work could have been finished long ere this. When God's power is released through the remnant church, this old world will be turned upside down.

It is not numbers that count. Rome trembled before the lone monk of Wittenberg. Queen Mary dreaded less the army of the nation than the fearless Knox, who stormed and shattered the stronghold of usurping tyranny. Garibaldi and one thousand men were enough to change the history of Italy. Gideon and three hundred men overthrew the hosts of Midian. Wesley said that if he could have a hundred men who feared nought but sin, he would shake the world. God give us those men. Then, minions of darkness, beware!

"There is nothing that Satan fears so much as that the people of God shall clear the way by removing every hindrance, so that the Lord can pour out His Spirit upon a languishing church and an impenitent congregation. . . . When the way is prepared for the Spirit of God, the blessing will come."—MRS. E. G. WHITE in *Review and Herald,* March 22, 1887.

When Moody was preaching in Chicago, two

women came to him and said, "We are praying for you."

"Praying for me?" he queried in surprise. "Why, am I not preaching the gospel? Why don't you pray for those who hear?"

They told him that he was preaching the gospel, *but without power.* The arrow went to its mark, and humbly he asked them to continue to pray for him. The whole world knows of the revolution that came into his life, "God's man in God's place doing God's work in God's way."

J. Wilbur Chapman was a successful pastor of a popular church. He was preaching to a great congregation with conspicuous eloquence. Moody visited him but was not impressed. He put his hand on Chapman's shoulder. "Do you know you are a failure here?" he asked. "You are making a mistake in your ministry. You are not winning souls. I say it in all brotherly kindness."

The rebuke wounded deeply. For weeks Chapman smarted under it. At last, on October 16, 1892, he cried, "O God, I am willing to be made willing about everything." And the world knows the result.

### The Sole Hope of the Remnant

Oh, who will stop some of us in our complacent course? We need to be arrested, gripped, startled. Do not avoid the issue by working harder. The point is not lack either of intensity or of extensity. Never was there so much work as there is today. It is not enough to stir people to be busy for Him. We must win souls. We must finish our twofold task. We need the fire of God in our souls. Where is our agony over souls in alienation against God? Where is our power to win them in Pentecostal numbers?

God is still waiting for the remnant band of men who will wholly surrender themselves to Him. And they are in this movement today.

"There is no limit to the usefulness of the one who, putting self aside, makes room for the working of the Holy Spirit upon his heart, and lives a life wholly consecrated to God."—*Testimonies,* vol. 8, p. 19.

Within thirty years after the cross the whole known world had been influenced by a handful of men. Today there are eight hundred million heathen, and multiplied millions of the nominal Christians in Babylon, having the form of godliness without the power. And oh, how many of us are starving on the surface of the richest mine in the universe of God, like the old man who owned three hundred acres, but was poor almost to starvation! One day men appeared and surveyed the land, asked the price, and paid him $1 an acre therefor. Yet out of that very land millions upon millions of dollars have been taken, and are still being taken. Its wealth seems unlimited. It is one of the richest mines in the world.

The tragedy of our poverty! And there are unclaimed, unlimited treasures awaiting us. The bankers of Scotland are said to have £40,000,000 in unclaimed deposit. But the riches of all heaven, in the Holy Spirit, await our demand and reception. We need not wait for others to claim. Let us go to God individually. And let us go as a church.

In Edinburgh stands the historic Greyfriar's church, surrounded by a mossy old graveyard. It was there that, several generations ago, a company of determined, solemn men signed the national covenant, the Earl of Sutherland leading the way. There they opened the veins of their arms and signed the covenant with their own blood.

Let us as heralds of our coming Lord open the throne rooms of our hearts, and bid Him enter for the finishing of His work in the world through us. It is the imperious call of the hour. And the need will be met by the coming of the men.

A number of years ago in the city of Charleston, there was a Negro, a wonderful chime player by the name of Gadsen, who played only as one could who made it truly a part of worship. When the city was shaken by an earthquake, terror and despair possessed all minds. Men were fleeing for their lives. The air was filled with the crash of falling buildings and the shrieks of the wounded. Gadsen rushed to his post, and sent pealing forth through the darkness the strains of "Rock of Ages," to hush and calm the hearts of men. It proved a mighty, steadying, assuring force.

In this time, when the foundations of faith are being shaken, when the hopes of men are perishing, when souls are filled with darkness and foreboding and doubt, and multitudes are crying for the sound of comfort and hope, God calls for His faithful bell ringers to peal out to church and world, "Holy Spirit, light divine." Let every man sound it forth!

> "Holy Spirit, light divine,
>      Shine upon this heart of mine,
> Chase the shades of night away,
>      Turn my darkness into day.
>
>          .    .    .    .    .
>
> "Holy Spirit, all divine,
>      Dwell within this heart of mine,
> Cast down every idol throne,
>      Reign supreme, and reign alone."

Part IV

*Symbols of the Spirit*

# ⤜⤜⤜⤜⤜⤜ *Burn in Me* ⤛⤛⤛⤛⤛⤛

BURN in me, fire of God,
   Burn till my heart is pure;
Burn till I love God fervently,
   Burn till my faith is sure.

Burn in me, fire of God,
   Burn deeper, deeper still;
Burn till my one and sole desire
   Shall be the Father's will.

Burn in me, fire of God,
   Burn though it cost me dear;
Burn till my wakened, quickened soul
   God's smallest whisper hear.

Burn in me, fire of God,
   Until within shall rise,
And out, and up to God's great throne
   A pleasing sacrifice.

Burn in me, fire of God,
   Yea, burn, and burn again,
Till all I am, by God consumed,
   A "flame of fire" remain.

                —PERCY G. PARKER.

❮❮❮❮❮❮❮❮❮❮❮❮❮❮❮

# CHAPTER FOURTEEN

# The Breath of the Almighty

WONDROUS are the ways of God, and matchless His provisions for the children of His love. By precept and promise, by fact and figure, He patiently discloses the plans and provisions of His grace—the Infinite meeting the limitations of our finite understanding. With unerring wisdom He uses symbols and types to make plain to the spiritually-minded the deep things that are but inscrutable mysteries to the natural mind. And the more important a truth or provision is for us, the greater the variety of approaches employed to clarify our understanding, to appeal to our minds, and to challenge our consciences.

God has expressly said of His methods: "I have ... used similitudes, by the ministry of the prophets." Hosea 12:10. Similitudes afford comparisons that make the realities represented vivid and living to mankind. Indeed, the Bible is largely a book of varying metaphors, similes, types, symbols, parables, allegories, and emblems. Unfigurative words are often lame vehicles of truth; but with words clothed in the robes of symbol—these figures of human speech and earthly imagery—truth is made gripping and real.

Even thus are the majestic operations of the Holy Spirit strikingly portrayed under the luminous symbols of fire, water, oil, and wind, each with its special emphasis and unique lessons. To say that the Holy Spirit is like wind in its operations and effects, expresses more than a whole chapter of unfigurative words could convey. Now the simple truth is that the Hebrew word *ruach,* and the Greek word *pneuma,* are translated not only *spirit* but *wind, air,* and *breath.* The context must determine the rendering. It is this curious fact of the language that probably gave rise to a deeply impressive symbolism; for wind is but air in motion, and breath is but a synonym for inbreathed life.

This emblem of the wind, or breath, signifying the comings and goings of the Holy Spirit, was illustrated *typically* in connection with the inbreathing of the breath of life into the first man, Adam, in Genesis 2:7; *prophetically* in the vision of the valley of dry bones and the vivifying wind in Ezekiel 37:1-10; and doctrinally in Christ's remarkable declaration to Nicodemus of the Spirit's operations in the new birth, recorded in John 3:3-8. These we shall study. The possible deductions awaiting recognition are many; but let us search for the more outstanding lessons, for like the Spirit, air is never idle.

### Is Essential to Life

First, air is essential to life. Surrounding the globe is a mighty ocean of air, or atmosphere, without which we could not live. Were it not for this, all would be desolation and death. It is absolutely necessary for all animal and vegetable life. The waves of this mighty ocean, which envelops us, sometimes roll over us in the rush of the tempest; at other times its murmurs lull us to sleep in its calm. But it is there, though invisible.

The air we breathe is one of the most necessary elements of nature. We can live a lifetime without sight, hearing, or speech; we can live for weeks without food, for days without water, but only for a few minutes without air. It is so identified with life that when we cease to breathe we cease to live. When a person drowns, the first-aid measures are to restore respiration. The lonely aviator in his altitude flights or the diver as he plumbs the depths, must each have his oxygen supply. The dying often have the same precious oxygen supplied as a last hope. Even fire refuses to burn without air.

This enveloping atmosphere is indispensable for the radiation of solar light and heat, and yet at the same time it forms a curtain of defense. Even so does the blessed Holy Spirit, symbolized by the wind, air, or breath—as variously expressed—bring the breath of life to the soul. It creates the atmosphere in which Christians live and move and have their being; by which we see and hear the things of God, and are thus enabled to dwell in the warm radiance of His love.

Coming now to the direct spiritual parallel of this

first point, note these scriptures: "The spirit of God hath made me, and the breath of the Almighty hath given me life." Job 33:4. Again: "Thou sendest forth Thy spirit, they are created" (Ps. 104:30); and, "By the word of the Lord were the heavens made; and all the host of them by the breath of His mouth" (Ps. 33:6). Once more: "All the while my breath is in me, and the spirit of God is in my nostrils." Job 27:3. Referring to the same facts and conditions, spirit and breath are thus used interchangeably, depending upon the literal or symbolic intent of the language. And mark well, it was the Spirit who was ever the divine agent in creation in giving life.

Allusion to the Spirit as the creative agency of the Godhead carries us back logically and inevitably to the days of creation as a starting point. Note first the sharp distinction between the creation of the animals and that of man. The lower animals sprang instantly into being at the creative word. But man, the crowning handiwork of God, was first formed of the dust of the earth. Yes, we are but common clay, and not gold dust, powdered pearls, or diamond dust. But man's frame was still lifeless until God kissed the cold lips with His own warm breath of life, and life was transmitted to the form of clay.

Here is the inspired (which means God-breathed) record: "The Lord God formed man of the dust of the ground, and breathed into his nostrils the breath of life; and man became a living soul." Gen.

2:7. This is the second allusion to the work of the Holy Spirit in the beginning of Scripture, the first being in the second verse of the first chapter—the earliest possible moment: "The earth was without form, and void; and darkness was upon the face of the deep. And the Spirit of God moved upon the face of the waters." The Spirit is ever and always the creative instrument. This fact, ever remembered, will explain His central relation to the universe, and will clarify a thousand mysteries.

Life came to Adam not as an animal impulse but by the "breath of the Almighty," in Job 33:4 and elsewhere it is plainly attributed to the Holy Spirit. The act of material formation was succeeded by inspiration, animation, and quickening. Let us then learn the lesson that not the material but the spiritual is the source of life, and that the Holy Spirit's highest work is the communication of new and supernatural life, whether in creation or re-creation.

Because of this we should sense the sacredness of the human body, and the value and importance of life, which is the direct result of the Holy Spirit's operation. Consequently, murder and suicide constitute a blow struck at God's own bestowed life. That is why it is a capital offense. Our life is to be held as a sacred gift, and our talents and endowments, whether the genius of a Milton, the art of a Raphael, or the music of a Mozart, are to be cherished as a solemn trust.

### Imperative for Our Regeneration

But alas, sin, has made its devastating inroads upon these human lives. Sin has brought pollution, separation, and death. Here again the Holy Spirit's work becomes necessary for restoration. The provision for our re-creation or regeneration presented by the apostle John, is so like this original picture in Genesis that the one seems, as it is, but the complement of the other. Indeed, regeneration is divinely declared to be a "new creation." Note this series of expressions: "Wherefore if any man is in Christ, there is a new creation." 2 Cor. 5:17, A.R.V., margin. "We are His workmanship, created in Christ Jesus." Eph. 2:10. Titus also speaks clearly of this renewing through the Holy Spirit. (Titus 3:5.)

This new birth, as it is called, was disclosed impressively by the Master to Nicodemus in John 3:5-8: "Jesus answered, Verily, verily, I say unto thee, Except a man be born of water and of the Spirit, he cannot enter into the kingdom of God. That which is born of the flesh is flesh; and that which is born of the Spirit is spirit. . . . The wind bloweth where it listeth, and thou hearest the sound thereof, but canst not tell whence it cometh, and whither it goeth: so is every one that is born of the Spirit." Such regeneration alone restores to man his forfeited spiritual life, which is supernatural and divine in origin. Of this silent, imperceptible, but powerful work, we read:

"Like the wind, which is invisible, yet the effects

of which are plainly seen and felt, is the Spirit of God in its work upon the human heart. That regenerating power, which no human eye can see, begets a new life in the soul; it creates a new being in the image of God. While the work of the Spirit is silent and imperceptible, its effects are manifest."—*Steps to Christ,* p. 61.

It was alone in the garden, as the soft night breezes laden with the fragrance of far-off fields fanned their faces, that Jesus in converse with Nicodemus seized upon this familiar symbol of the wind to force home a mighty truth. As already stated, both in the Hebrew which Jesus used in His conversation with Nicodemus, and in the Greek in which John recorded it, the words for spirit, breath, and wind are similar in meaning. It is this that gives rise to the analogies of the text. But if Jesus wanted to use a symbol for Spirit here, why did not He so state it? Now that is precisely what He did. In the original, the text reads, "born of *water* and of *wind*," a couplet of symbols.

This usual meaning of wind is confirmed by the usual accompanying verb, "bloweth," and the explanatory expression, "sound." But by universal consent wind, or *pneuma* (from *to breathe* or *blow,* and occurring 370 times in the New Testament), is here translated Spirit. In verse 8 we note the alternative rendering: "The Spirit breatheth where it will." A.R.V., margin; also Rotherham and Douay. In our common version the symbolic name "the wind" occurs. So the operation of the Spirit is the one transcendent factor in regeneration, indispensable for every soul that shall ever see the kingdom of heaven. The Spirit is the begetter and sustainer of the new life. He is undeniably God's quickening agent.

The other symbol, "water," is at once a reference to water baptism, and to the cleansing, renewing power of the "word," which is the other instrument in regeneration. Thus we read: "Being born again . . . by the word of God." 1 Peter 1:23. "Of His own will begat He us with the word of truth." James 1:18. Frequently in Scripture water and its cleansing work are used to symbolize the word. So we read: "That He might sanctify and cleanse it with the washing of water by the word" (Eph. 5:26); "now ye are clean through the word which I have spoken unto you" (John 15:3).

Thus God works through the Holy Spirit, and the Holy Spirit through the instrumentality of the Word. It is the same combined interworking of Word ("God said," Gen. 1:3, 6, 9, etc.) and Spirit (which "moved," Gen. 1:2), as in the original creation, that effects the new birth.

### Prerequisite for All Service

Another remarkable counterpart of the Genesis record is presented in John 20:21-23: "Then said Jesus to them again, Peace be unto you: as My Father hath sent Me, even so send I you. And when He had said this, He breathed on them, and saith unto them, Receive ye the Holy Ghost: whose soever sins ye remit, they are remitted unto them; and whose soever sins ye retain, they are retained." Jesus was about to invest them with their sacred commission, to equip them with the indispensable power, and to unfold to them the solemn issues of their work.

When He first appeared unto them after His resurrection, He said, "Peace be unto you." Verse 19. That first bestowal of peace was for the restoration of their confidence. This second bestowal of "peace," in verse 21, is a preparation for their work. Solemnly He pronounces the charge, making them His envoys. His authority is here disclosed as equal with that of the Father.

It was not a new work to which they were called. As He was the light of the world, so were they to be; as He came to seek and to save the lost, so were they to go; as His meat was to do the Father's will, so theirs was to be; and as He was filled with the Spirit and spake and wrought only through the Spirit, even so must they be and do. Only thus could they discharge their weighty trust. No man is qualified to minister, no matter what his earthly credentials, unless he has this enduement of the Holy Spirit. Much so-called Christian effort comes largely to nought simply because of this precise lack.

It should be observed in passing that this investment did not make superfluous the further gift of the Holy Spirit in His fullness on the day of Pentecost; rather, it was anticipatory.

By the same authority which had been exercised in commissioning the disciples, Jesus now bequeathed to them the Holy Spirit. The act was symbolic, after the manner of the Hebrew prophets in ancient times. This symbolic action reminds one again instinctively of the creation record. "Breathed" is the same word used in Genesis 2:7. Indeed, Jesus was the same one who breathed life into Adam's nostrils, as we know. In both instances He inbreathed His own spirit, which was thus imparted to them. "Spirit of God" (Gen. 1:2), "Spirit of Christ" (Rom. 8:9), and "Spirit of Jesus" (Acts 16:7, A.R.V.), are but alternative names for the Holy Spirit. They are synonymous, and are used interchangeably in Scripture. Thus Christ connects the Holy Spirit inseparably with Himself.

Even so are we taught never to try to obtain the Holy Spirit apart from Jesus, but through fellowship with Him. May this basic truth be burned into our consciousness forever! We read from the Spirit of prophecy:

"Our people need the breath of life breathed into them, that they may arouse to spiritual action. Many have lost their vital energy; they are sluggish, dead, as it were. Let those who have been receiving the grace of Christ help these souls to arouse to action.

Let us keep in the current of life that comes from Christ, that we may kindle life in some other soul."—MRS. E. G. WHITE in *Review and Herald,* April 28, 1904.

It will be observed also that the same word is found here—"breath" or "wind"—that was used by Jesus in His conversation with Nicodemus. (John 3:8.) "The *wind* bloweth where it listeth," or "the Spirit *breatheth* where it will." A.R.V., margin. This identity in language further identifies the Spirit's work.

Another related point that should be observed here is that the word "receive" is otherwise rendered "take ye" the Holy Gift. They were not to be wholly passive. Through this enduement, then, were they qualified for the work they were to do. Never are men equipped or authorized to represent Christ without first receiving the life-giving Spirit of Jesus.

The Spirit's coming may be quiet as an evening zephyr, as in this experience; or mighty as the tempest's power, as in its fullness at Pentecost. It may be as the murmuring whisper of the still small voice, or as the tornado's roar. The accompaniments matter little; it is the reality that counts. Think of the Aeolian harp, with its strings arranged in musical harmony. As the wind passes over them they seem touched as by unseen fingers, and notes almost divine float out over the air. It is as if a choir of angels touched the strings. Ah, let us keep our heartstrings open to the almost imperceptible touch of the Spirit, that we too many give forth the music of heaven.

This Spirit of prophecy comment on John 20:22 will be pertinent here:

"The Holy Spirit was not yet fully manifested; for Christ had not yet been glorified. The more abundant impartation of the Spirit did not take place till after Christ's ascension. Not until this was received could the disciples fulfil the commission to preach the gospel to the world. But the Spirit was now given for a special purpose. Before the disciples could fulfil their official duties in connection with the church, Christ breathed His Spirit upon them. He was committing to them a most sacred trust, and He desired to impress them with the fact that without the Holy Spirit this work could not be accomplished.

"The Holy Spirit is the breath of spiritual life in the soul. The impartation of the Spirit is the impartation of the life of Christ. It imbues the receiver with the attributes of Christ. Only those who are thus taught of God, those who possess the inward working of the Spirit, and in whose life the Christ-life is manifested, are to stand as representative men, to minister in behalf of the church."—*The Desire of Ages,* p. 805.

May it never be forgotten that this was requisite before the disciples could fulfill their official duties. Only those today who have the Spirit breathed upon them are fitted and qualified for service in the church as we await the mighty fullness of power of the Spirit in the loud cry of the approaching last-day Pentecost.

### Invisible in Its Essence

A second lesson from the wind is that it is invisible in its essence. But its invisibility does not do away with its actuality. The voiceless, unseen wind is known, not by visible perception, but by its powerful effects which are manifest. It turns the windmill. It propels the ship. In John 3:8 a comparison is established between the unseen presence of the wind and the invisible operations of the Holy Spirit in regeneration. The "sound" that is heard is the only evidence in addition to its observable effects. An impenetrable veil of mystery is drawn about the Spirit's person and His visitations. His operations are always hidden; but His presence is discoverable by the results. And praise God, we can receive His life, love, purity, peace, power, and joy.

More than that, we can hear the sound of His "voice," though His comings and goings are concealed. This comes within range of our own conscious experience. How oft He has spoken, directing the thought and conscience to the word and counsel of God. But have we always heeded? If we persist in ignoring or flouting His voice, then finally after sound comes silence.

Clearly the Master tells it, speaking of the "Spirit of truth; whom the world cannot receive, because it seeth Him not, neither knoweth Him: but ye know Him; for He dwelleth with you, and shall be in you." John 14:17. Where He is received, He is perceived. And to *know* Him is to be swayed by His will, to be inspired by His love, kept by His grace, led by His hand, sustained by His power, and used in His service. Blessed provision of the Spirit of God!

### Mysterious in Its Action

The third lesson is that the wind is mysterious in its action. Its movements are beyond our direction or control. With incomparable majesty it chooses its own pathway. None can foresee with certainty its course. It drives the clouds of heaven hither and yon, and tosses the ocean waves into heaps. It rocks the bird in her nest. It bends the forest beneath the rushing wheels of the whirlwind's chariot. It sweeps the desert as with the burning blast of a furnace, and lashes with its cutting breath the fur-clad denizens of the North until they cry out with agony.

The wind is constantly used as a symbol of freedom. "Free as the wind," is a common expression. Air in action is less trammeled than any other force at work in the realm of nature.

The apostle John says it "bloweth where it *listeth*." *Listeth* comes from the Greek *theleo*, meaning "willeth" or "chooseth." It is the same word that is used in 1 Corinthians 4:19, "If the Lord *will*"; and Philippians 2:13, "To *will* and to do." The Holy

Spirit, symbolized by the wind, acts in the sovereignty of His grace. Though we know many things about Him, we cannot anticipate or regulate His operations. Rather, *He* divides "to every man severally as He will." 1 Cor. 12:11. It is for us to yield to His power and to come into harmony with His operations.

Yes, the Spirit is mysterious in His action. He is not limited by human laws and expectations. The Spirit falls on an Augustinian monk, and shakes all Europe. He touches a tinker in Bedford jail, and *Pilgrim's Progress* springs forth. He lays His hand on a cobbler in Hackleton, and modern missions result. Aye, He is mysterious in His working.

We cannot escape from the presence of the Spirit of the Almighty. "Whither shall I go from Thy spirit? or whither shall I flee from Thy presence? If I ascend up into heaven, Thou art there: if I make my bed in hell, behold, Thou art there. If I take the wings of the morning, and dwell in the uttermost parts of the sea; even there shall Thy hand lead me, and Thy right hand shall hold me." Ps. 139:7-10. Though terrifying to the sinner how comforting is this to one who is seeking to do His will!

No more can the mystery of the new birth be explained than the mystery of the natural birth. Note this reference to the inscrutable ways of the wind in this connection: "As thou knowest not what is the way of the wind, nor how the bones do grow in the womb of her that is with child; even so thou knowest not the work of God who doeth all." Eccl. 11:5, A.R.V.

Think of Pentecost. The work of the Spirit, under the similitude of the "wind," was not a natural but a supernatural phenomenon. Forget not that it was "from heaven." (Acts 2:2.) Two symbols were used, one appealing to the hearing and the other to the sight, though the Spirit Himself was unseen and unheard. The wind would inevitably remind them of Jesus' well-known teaching to Nicodemus concerning the operation of the Spirit.

It would also remind them of the Old Testament pledge of God's presence as indicated to David by "the sound of a going in the tops of the mulberry trees" (2 Sam. 5:24); and in the expression of the psalmist, "who maketh winds His messengers." Ps. 104:4, A.R.V. Yes, they instantly recognized the symbol and rejoiced in the reality.

### Tremendous in Its Power

How tremendous the power wrapped up in the winds of heaven! No more forceful figure could be used to represent the resistless energy of the Almighty Spirit. There are "diversities of operations," but the same Spirit. (1 Cor. 12:6.) Sometimes they are manifested in gentleness; at other times, in power. It was so at Pentecost. Like the roar of a mighty tempest rushing toward them, it sweeps nearer until it bursts into the chamber. It was the old symbolism in vivid action, which lies in the very word *spirit.* Thus were poor, ignorant, inexperienced, jealous, and distrustful men transformed into veritable giants for God.

And Pentecost reversed Babel. Then were they of "one heart." It reminds us of 2 Chronicles 5:13: "It came even to pass, as the trumpeters and singers were as *one,* to make *one* sound to be heard in praising and thanking the Lord; and when they lifted up their voice with the trumpets and cymbals and instruments of musick, and praised the Lord, saying, For He is good; for His mercy endureth for ever: that *then* the house was filled with a cloud, even the house of the Lord." Yes, what we need is the Pentecostal Spirit, which alone will bring Pentecostal results.

The breath of God converted a mechanical organization into a living organism, a congregation into a church. It transformed that disciple band, honeycombed with envy and jealousy, into a spiritual army that could not be checked; for the Spirit endues people with power that makes them irresistible in life and service. Note this:

"There is a great work to do; and the Spirit of the living God must enter into the living messenger, that the truth may go with power."—MRS. E. G. WHITE in *Review and Herald,* Dec. 3, 1908.

They were all "filled" with the Holy Spirit. But one must be emptied before he can be filled. Air rushes in to fill a vacuum. We are filled when, by the abdication of self, we provide a vacuum. The infilling breath is dependent upon the previous exhalation. Note these impressive words:

"It is not enough to make the heart empty; we must have the vacuum filled with the love of God. The soul must be furnished with the graces of the Spirit of God. We may leave off bad habits, and yet not be truly sanctified, because we do not have a connection with God. We must unite with Christ. There is a reservoir of power at our command, and we are not to remain in the dark, cold, sunless cave of unbelief; or we shall not catch the bright beams of the Sun of Righteousness."—*Ibid.,* Jan. 24, 1893.

And let us also learn this golden secret: Pentecostal blessing is always preceded by Pentecostal prayer. Where the conditions have been met, the history of humanity ever since Pentecost has been one long, glorious commentary on the words of Acts 2. The mighty, melting, vivifying, purifying breath of God has swept like the warm south wind down upon a glacier in the spring, melting the thick-ribbed ice and wooing forth the fragrant flowers, even under its very shadows.

### Varied in Its Effects

Fourth, the wind is varied in its effects. It refreshes the faint, and restores the consumptive. It heals and develops strength, on the one hand; yet it also withers and blasts and brings destruction under other conditions. These strange anomalies will be reconciled as we study further its characteristics. It would take 800,000,000 horses working day and night to transport the water which the wind brings from the sea into the State of Pennsylvania alone—and all without the groaning of a wheel or the turning of a crank. Even so does the Holy Spirit minister to both the good and the evil. What a boon is this to both saint and sinner! But in the symbol much depends upon man's relationship to the wind.

In the Bahamas there are trade winds—months of a steady rush of wind that never varies. Likewise, there are the "trade winds" of the ever-moving breath of the Holy Spirit. O soul, get into the trade winds of God's love. Let them regenerate you, or revive you, as the need may be. Seek salvation, seek power, seek strength. All that you need has been provided. Then there are circuits in the wind's sovereign course: "The wind goeth toward the south, and turneth about unto the north; it whirleth about continually, and the wind returneth again according to his circuits." Eccl. 1:6. And there are special circuits in the Holy Spirit's operations, inclosing in His love, infolding in His presence, and encompassing in His power those who so yield to Him. How are we relating ourselves to these currents? The question is vital and pertinent.

> "One ship drives east and another drives west
> With the selfsame winds that blow.
> 'Tis the set of the sails
> And not the gales
> Which tells us the way to go."

## It Cleanses and Heals

Then, wind cleanses. In Job 37:21 we read of how "the wind passeth, and cleanseth." Yes, the Holy Spirit brings purity. And how we need it! The wind winnows and separates the chaff from the wheat, the false from the true. This searching, withering work of the Spirit is told in Isaiah 40:6, 7: "The voice said, Cry. And he said, What shall I cry?" Now comes the answer: "All flesh is grass, and all the goodliness thereof is as the flower of the field: the grass withereth, the flower fadeth: because the Spirit of the Lord bloweth upon it: surely the people is grass." It humbles and abases.

The operation of the Spirit caused Job to say, "I am vile" (Job 40:4), and David to cry, "I am a worm" (Ps. 22:6). It led Isaiah to protest, "I am a man of unclean lips" (Isa. 6:5); Paul to say, "I am carnal" (Rom. 7:14); and Peter to confess, "I am a sinful man" (Luke 5:8). But it blights and withers only that it may bless and ennoble. It humbles that it may exalt, and brings low that it may lift high.

Yes, the same blessed Spirit brings health and healing. Have you ever had the sensation of stifling or suffocating in a closed room? And have you then thrown open the windows and inhaled the fresh air? Ah, we need the open-air treatment for the suffocating, the sick, and the enfeebled. Come, ye sin-sick souls, into the great open spaces! Yea, more than that. Have you ever stood on a mountain peak near some great city lying in the valley hard by? Have you looked down upon the murky lowland with its smoky haze, its polluted atmosphere, its poisonous gases, and its noxious odors? Have you reveled in the freedom, the freshness, and the invigoration of the mountain air?

Oh, the splendor of the highlands! Come up from the murky lowlands, up where you can draw deep, full breaths of pure, vitalizing air. How it sends the lifeblood tingling through the entire circulatory system! All of which is a parable, for the air is a chosen emblem of the Spirit. We Christians need to practice deep breathing in the highlands of God. We need the Holy Spirit.

"We must rise above the frosty atmosphere in which we have hitherto lived, and with which Satan would surround our souls, and breathe in the hallowed atmosphere of heaven."—*Ibid.,* May 6, 1890.

We must have the reality suggested by this symbolic wind. See a beautiful ship with sails all set and anchor weighed. But there is no ripple by its side, no foam at its bow, and no progress. Why?—No wind! Or perhaps it is a becalmed sailing ship, caught on the mighty bosom of the ocean. There is a spot in the Atlantic called the Sargasso Sea, subject to long-continued calms and covered with thick, entangling weeds. Nothing used to strike the sailors with such dread as to be caught in that region. It was worse than any storm.

Unable to proceed, water gone, food exhausted, hope departing, and death facing the crew—how they long and pray for wind! With what joy the becalmed sailors see the ripple on the water in the distance and watch their sagging canvas bulge in response to the rising breeze! Oh, do we sense our need, and welcome as eagerly the Spirit's approach? This intense thirst for the Spirit is one of the paramount needs of the church today.

### Differs in His Operations

The wind is varied in its direction and in its actions. After sin had entered Eden, our first parents soon heard the seeking voice of God borne by the evening wind, calling, "Where art thou?" It was the voice of mercy, entreaty, and love. Just so in this our forfeited paradise; on the wings of the "wind" are borne to us the wooing overtures of God. And we can no more hide from Him now than could Adam then. Do we hear Him calling us now through the Holy Spirit? Then let us instantly heed.

Next, after the Deluge, God caused a mighty wind to blow upon the face of the flood, and the waters went back to the bed of the sea, and the ancient bounds were set again. The wind tore the misty veil from the mountains and dried the earth, preparing it for habitation again. Even as in the days of Noah, so before the coming of the Son of man, the mighty power of the Holy Spirit is to be exhibited in fitting and preparing these body temples of ours for His abode. How we need to understand and experience His work in the "loud cry" of this message. It is absolutely indispensable to our fitness for our eternal habitations.

Again, when Moses led the emigrating host of Israel out of Egypt, God blew upon the sea (Ex. 15:8, 10), and plowed a course for the deliverance of His people. Even so, by the work of the Spirit will our deliverance be wrought out in this world of sin. Our only hope lies in His miraculous work, and not in our genius or efforts. How tragic that we are so prone to forget this.

The Holy Spirit is varied in His operations. In Palestine there sometimes comes an *east wind* known as "sirocco," meaning poisoned wind, bringing calamity in its wake. It dries the throat, produces bronchial troubles, and creates oppressiveness. It was such an east wind that blasted Pharaoh's corn. (Gen. 41:6, 23, 27.) It was such that brought the locusts upon Egypt (Ex. 10:13) and that broke the ships of Tarshish (Ps. 48:7).

Sometimes the Holy Spirit comes as an east wind, breaking and distressing. "Will you pray for me?" asked a woman. "Yes, what for?" responded her minister. "I want patience." "O Lord, send this sister a lot of trials and persecution——" he began. "Stop!" she cried, "I don't want tribulation." Yet tribulation worketh patience.

Then there is the *west wind* of deliverance, which took the Egyptian locusts away. (Ex. 10:19.) So, at other times the Holy Spirit brings relief and grace and refreshing for our weariness. His name is the Comforter.

And there is the *north wind* for clearing (Prov. 25:23) and fair weather (Job 37:22). After clouds and storm the Holy Spirit brings the fair weather and the blue skies of hallowed communion.

The last of the four winds is the *south wind* of pleasantness that quiets the waters (Job 37:17), and brings forth fragrance (Song of Solomon 4:16). Felt at Joppa between nine and ten in the morning and reaching Jerusalem between two and three in the afternoon, there is a wind which subsides at sunset but rises again through the night, bathing, cooling, and refreshing the face of nature.

Its fragrance is its distinctive feature. Yes, the Holy Spirit releases sweet, refreshing odors—the frankincense of a consecrated life, the spikenard of love's devotion, the incense of grateful worship, the fragrance of adoring prayer, and the aroma of a holy character. Such are suggestions of His operations.

> "Lord, let Thy love
> Fresh from above,
> Soft as the south wind blow;
> Call forth its bloom,
> Wake its perfume,
> And bid its spices flow."

### Irresistible in Its Movements

Fifth, the wind is irresistible in its movements. Think of its matchless power. Who can stop it? See it stir and lash the ponderous ocean into violent fury until its crested waves are lifted into mountains. See it tear up the mighty giants of the forest like the tender plants of your garden. Watch it wreck the proudest monuments of man, bringing a great city to ruins, crushing its buildings like fragile toys. It is irresistible. Armies may seek in vain to stop its work. Lawmakers and jurists may pass their decrees against it. But though nations perish, legislators die, and their decrees are soon forgotten, the majestic wind sweeps on!

The wind, though invisible, is as actual as the ground we tread. It can be compressed into liquid form until it becomes more powerful than dynamite. In the Orient it is still customary to speak of the winds as "God's messengers."

A traveler and his Arab guide were riding their camels across the trackless desert when the guide commanded his companion to dismount and meet "God's messengers." As the Occidental traveler turned, he saw a suffocating cloud of dust raised by the hot winds sweeping down upon them with the speed of a hurricane. They had barely time to dismount and prostrate themselves upon the earth, covering their heads, before the cloud of dust was upon them, sifting through their clothing, and even caus-

ing the camels to moan under the intolerable misery
of suffocation.

Impressive and awful at times are the Holy
Spirit's manifestations of His presence and power. He
is sovereign in His operations. None can stand in
His way. Saints are melted, sinners are crushed; consciences are quickened, and holy feelings are stirred;
bitterness is expelled, wrongs are righted, and resti-
tutions made. Under the intensity of His humbling
power, secret sins are confessed, and unholy ambition,
impurity, prayerlessness, and neglect of the Bible
are forsaken. He does not toss us about in unavailing
contortions, but works glorious, intelligent results.

While the hurricane spreads devastation and
death on the one hand, the workings of the Holy
Spirit bring deliverance and life on the other hand, if
we respond to His operations. Pentecost saw a "rushing mighty wind." Each word is significant. *Wind* is
from the Greek word *pnoe,* from which we get *respiration, breathe,* and *blow.* Thus reference is clearly
made to the act of a living Person, the same who at
creation breathed into the silent form and transformed it into a living soul, and who before His
ascension breathed power upon the disciples as He
commissioned them His representatives in the world.

*Mighty* denotes vital activity, whirling, thunder-
ing, and moving in majesty. And *rushing* denotes
carrying speed, as a ship is driven before a storm. So
the Spirit has power to breathe, to move, to bring.

As a result of His visitation at Pentecost, the disciples had power in utterance—"all . . . began to speak." And their utterance produced profound conviction— their hearers were "pricked in their heart."

Under the same Spirit's inspiration men of old spoke the words of God as they were borne along under the mighty impetus of His power. (2 Peter 1:21.) Let us bow our heads in awe and reverence in the presence of Him who is omnipotent. There is nothing too hard for Him. May humble submission to Him not be too hard for us.

### A Vision of the Spirit's Power

In closing this search into the treasuries of the wind, let us study perhaps the most remarkable presentation of the life-giving power of the Spirit in the midst of utter hopelessness disclosed in the Word. It is found in Ezekiel's vision of the valley of dry bones. We read first the Inspired Record:

"The hand of the Lord was upon me, and carried me out in the spirit of the Lord, and set me down in the midst of the valley which was full of bones, and caused me to pass by them round about: and, behold, there were very many in the open valley; and, lo, they were very dry. And He said unto me, Son of man, can these bones live? And I answered, O Lord God, Thou knowest. Again He said unto me, Prophesy upon these bones, and say unto them, O ye dry bones, hear the word of the Lord. Thus saith the

Lord God unto these bones; Behold, I will cause breath to enter into you, and ye shall live: and I will lay sinews upon you, and will bring up flesh upon you, and cover you with skin, and put breath in you, and ye shall live; and ye shall know that I am the Lord.

"So I prophesied as I was commanded: and as I prophesied, there was a noise, and behold a shaking, and the bones came together, bone to his bone. And when I beheld, lo, the sinews and the flesh came up upon them, and the skin covered them above: but there was no breath in them. Then said He unto me, Prophesy unto the wind, prophesy, son of man, and say to the wind, Thus saith the Lord God; Come from the four winds, O breath, and breathe upon these slain, that they may live. So I prophesied as He commanded me, and the breath came into them, and they lived, and stood up upon their feet, an exceeding great army." Eze. 37:1-10.

The scene is laid in an ancient open valley, strewn with a disintegrating heap of human bones, the skeletons of a fallen army. Ezekiel's attention is engrossed by two facts—their number and their condition. These were not minimized. They were *"very* many" and *"very* dry." Exposed to wind and rain, bleached and whitened, every vestige of life had disappeared. Gone was the marrow within as well as the flesh without. It was a spectacle of desolation. How hopeless all seemed. As far as natural resources were concerned, despair seemed rational, and reanimation an impossibility. But his own powerlessness did not make the prophet despondent, for "with God all things are possible."

"Son of man, can these bones live?" was the question propounded to the prophet. At an earlier time in his life he might have rashly answered, "No, of course not!" But he had learned to know God's power. And his wise answer was, "Lord God, Thou knowest." No man could accomplish it, but God could. Then Ezekiel was commanded to prophesy unto the bones. He was taught the agency by which God will effect His purpose. He received not only an answer, but a message.

To prophesy is to predict what is to come to pass, to declare the will of God. He was to preach the Word of God to these dry bones. But how could these dry bones hear? Ah, because it was not the word of man but the word of God that he proclaimed. So he speaks over them the divine promises. His word pierces the ear of the dead. Observe, as we proceed, how the vision follows the precise order of the original creation—first the formation of the body, and afterward the inspiring breath of life. And note again the inseparable union of word and Spirit as in the original creation.

And while Ezekiel was still speaking, he was sensible of the effect of his words. There was a commotion among the bones. Movement supplanted the morbid stillness. There was the noise of a shaking as bone moved toward bone, until complete skeletons were formed. Sinews appeared and tied the bones together. Flesh filled the hollows, and muscles came into place prepared to give action. The organs were all there, but life was wanting. They have the forms of men, but there they lie prostrate—a host of corpses! And there the process of restoration in the first episode ends.

Herein lies a lesson: Ezekiel's prophesying directly to the bones brought a certain physical reconstruction and movement, but that was all. Man's teachings to man produce certain outward changes, reformations, and improvements; but man cannot give life. Such would be the effect of the word apart from the Spirit, were they to be separated. And this explains an abortive evangelistic endeavor.

But in the second phase of the vision the prophet is commanded to address the wind, or "Spirit" (R.V., margin). Then follows his great invocation, the entreaty of command, and under the living breath of the wind, or Spirit, there is an amazing spectacle. See the quivering movement as life passes into their frames, and they spring to their feet. It is the vivifying ministry of the Spirit that is here portrayed. The effect is not simply reformation but transformation and animation. It is an impressive manifestation of the Spirit's divine presence and operation. The expression, "four winds," recognizes, of course, His omnipresence in the world.

## The Personal Application

The vision is figurative, but the actuality is real. Though it applied nationally to Israel, its wider application is to men dead in trespasses and sins. Far worse than the death of a nation, as such, is the death of a soul. And God reckons us all as dead, separated from Him, until and unless reanimated by His Spirit. The figure is perfect. We are very many and very dry. Hope lies prostrate—from a human viewpoint. But, bless God, even the dead hear the words of God. The human agency, too, is emphasized as essential. But its limitations must be recognized. And the breath of the Almighty is our hope.

There is here the same twofold agency. First, the Word of God is the divine instrument in the conversion of souls. But the Word alone does not put the breath of life into the soul. The great agent in living transformation and transfiguration from the death of sin to a life of righteousness is the Holy Spirit.

The Holy Spirit's highest office is to enkindle new life in the dead. Blessed power! A corpse may be subjected to a galvanic current, and so produce muscular movements. It may simulate life through motion, but it has no life, notwithstanding the familiar motions. The vital spark is lacking. It must have life—derived and bestowed life—from the Source of life, or it remains a corpse, and disintegration is inevitable.

This is essential for us to remember along with

our needful activities. There is no work of restoration too hard for God. How good that is! And as we have a resurrective God, even so we need a resurrective faith. We need, we want, we must have, life, the Spirit, the breath of the Almighty. Read these gripping words from the Spirit of prophecy:

"The Spirit of God, with its vivifying power, must be in every human agent, that every spiritual muscle and sinew may be in exercise. Without the Holy Spirit, without the breath of God, there is torpidity of conscience, loss of spiritual life. Many who are without spiritual life have their names on the church records, but they are not written in the Lamb's book of life. They may be joined to the church, but they are not united to the Lord. They may be diligent in the performance of a certain set of duties, and may be regarded as living men; but many are among those who 'have a name that thou livest, and art dead.' Unless there is genuine conversion of the soul to God; unless the vital breath of God quickens the soul to spiritual life; unless the professors of truth are actuated by heaven-born principle, they are not born of the incorruptible seed which liveth and abideth forever. Unless they trust in the righteousness of Christ as their only security; unless they copy His character, labor in His spirit, they are naked, they have not on the robe of His righteousness. The dead are often made to pass for the living; for those who are working out what they term salvation after their own ideas, have not God working in them to will and to do of His good pleasure. This class is well represented by the valley of dry bones Ezekiel saw in vision. Those who have had committed to them the treasures of truth, and yet who are dead in trespasses and sin, need to be created anew in Christ Jesus."— Mrs. E. G. White in *Review and Herald,* Jan. 17, 1893.

Go to a church. Perhaps it is handsomely appointed, with a fine choir, a gifted preacher, and a service well arranged—but all form; there is no spirit, no life. A church may be perfectly organized and yet be perfectly dead. Months pass. You return to the same church, but there is a new power in the singing, a new grip in the preaching. It throbs with life. Why? The breath of God has blown upon it.

And just such miracles do occur. The same is more often true with individuals. May God teach us from the treasuries of the wind the indispensability of the Holy Spirit for life and service and victory. It is our sole hope of triumph. We must have His resurrection life in the midst of abounding death. And the blessed work is under way. God's Word will not return unto Him void; and His glorious provision will not fail.

Come, Breath of divine life and love, breathe into these barren, desert hearts of ours. Yea, we crave not simply a breath, but a "mighty rushing wind"— Thine energizing self. Grant it, Lord Jesus.

# CHAPTER FIFTEEN

# Rivers of Living Water

"IN THE last day, that great day of the feast, Jesus stood and cried, saying, If any man thirst, let him come unto Me, and drink. He that believeth on Me, as the scripture hath said, out of his belly shall flow rivers of living water. (But this spake He of the Spirit, which they that believe on Him should receive: for the Holy Ghost was not yet given; because that Jesus was not yet glorified.)" John 7:37-39.

The Feast of Tabernacles, at which these words were uttered, was the last of the three annual feasts of the Jews, and came toward the close of the year. Next to the Passover, it was the most impressive of the great national solemnities of the Hebrews. The inhabitants from far and near, and many from beyond the confines of Palestine, gathered at Jerusalem for this great convocation, which lasted eight days and was the memorial of God's protecting care and supplying grace during the days of their wanderings in the wilderness.

It commemorated their tent life; so they dwelt in booths made from the green boughs or branches of trees, spending the week in the open air. The first seven days typified their life in the wilderness, but the eighth memorialized their entrance into the

Promised Land; hence, upon that day they forsook these booths and returned to their own houses. The streets and courts, the housetops and lanes, the hills and vales, of Jerusalem and its environs were dotted with these picturesque booths. So thick were they that they gave the appearance of a veritable forest of palm and pine, olive and myrtle. Every Israelite was arrayed in his best attire, and each carried a green palm branch.

At night the city was illuminated by myriad lights. The Temple court especially was a blaze of light, and the eyes of all were directed there. This lies back of Christ's clarion challenge, "I am the light of the world." He would redirect their attention to Himself as the light "which lighteth every man that cometh into the world."

Each day at dawn, a vast procession wended its way to the Valley of the Kidron, headed by the officiating priest, who filled a golden pitcher from the Pool of Siloam, which is fed by living springs. This golden beaker he lifted to his shoulder, and keeping time to the choral music with slow, measured tread, he chanted, "Our feet shall stand within thy gates, O Jerusalem" (Ps. 122:2), as he led the procession onward and upward. Climbing the steep ascent of Mount Moriah, he passed through the Water Gate, up the broad stairs of the Temple court, and stopped before the altar, at the base of which were silver funnels connected with conduits leading under the

Temple to the Kidron, and thence to the Dead Sea.

In the time of Christ, as the four hundred priests sang the great Hallel, the people prayed, "Save us, we beseech Thee, O God." Then the officiating priest cried, "With joy shall ye draw water out of the wells of salvation" (Isa. 12:3), as he poured the consecrated water into one of the funnels, thus typifying the fount that gushed from the rock to quench the thirst of the Israelites. At the close of the festive sacrifices the priests formed a procession and, singing, made a circuit of the altar.

### The Empty Pitcher Lifted

Now, this ceremony was performed daily for the first seven days, visualizing the promise of living water that was to flow from Jerusalem. On the eighth day, called the last day or great day of the feast, the day of hosannas and the waving of branches, this libation of water was not offered. Instead, there was a simple ceremony of lifting the empty pitcher, raised to high heaven in mute appeal by the officiating priest. It was an eloquent expression of the unfulfilled promises and unsatisfied longings of the Jewish church and nation.

The seventh day, just preceding this great last day, was the climax of festivity and exhausting joy. The priests marched seven times instead of but once in connection with this final libation of water. By this time the people were worn out with singing and shouting. Joy had become wearisome. The reaction of faintness and exhaustion was overpowering. There was nothing more to interest or excite.

The people were perplexed and bewildered. Their hearts were yearning and craving for something, though they did not understand what. For in it all there was nothing for the soul—nothing in the scenes of pomp, nothing in the rounds of festivity, the dazzling light, the tuneful music. And Jesus' great heart of love was touched with their need and their recognized feeling of want. That love comprehends our needs and longings today.

It was on that last day, just as the priest elevated the empty pitcher and a great hush of somber silence had fallen over the multitude, that Jesus stood and cried, in a clear, ringing voice, "If any man thirst, let him come unto Me and drink. He that believeth on Me, as the scripture hath said, from within him shall flow rivers of living water. But this spake He of the Spirit, which they that believed on Him were to receive." John 7:37-39, A.R.V.

One can imagine the tremendous, almost electric effect. What an offer on such a day, in such a place, under such circumstances, and to such a congregation! Never did Jesus make a stronger appeal to man's sense of need. They knew the voice, and felt the strange power of the invitation. And in the nineteen hundred years that have passed, those words have not lost their magnetic power.

### The Thirst of the Human Spirit

The deep cravings of the human spirit are well expressed by the figure "thirst," and their eternal satisfaction by the expression, "drink." Hear Him: "If any man"—the poorest, the lowest, the worst, the richest, the highest, the best. All are invited. How good Jesus is to thirsty souls! Ah, there is an inner thirst as truly as there is an inner man, and that thirst is greater and deeper than the physical thirst of the body.

The cry of the wounded soldier lying on the battlefield is not for relief from pain but for *water, water.* The cry of the storm-tossed sailor after days of drifting in the lifeboat is not for food but for *water, water.* The cry of the martyr in his slow death is not for relief from anguish but for *water, water.* Even the Christ Himself on the cross cried, "I thirst." And it was just after He had said, "My God, My God, why hast Thou forsaken Me?"

The thirst of the body is a fit symbol of the soul without God, a life devoid of the Holy Spirit. For "this spake He of the Spirit." No language can describe, no imagination conceive, the destitution of man without a Saviour. The cry of the sin-scorched heart of humanity is for the water that is here held forth, that alone can quench the thirst of the soul. But how often the cry of weariness and woe is stifled by plunging into a thousand and one alleviating devices that only aggravate the trouble.

I wonder whether we really do thirst? Do we feel a real drought of the soul? Do we recognize our imperative need? I solemnly affirm that if we think we can get along without the living water, we shall not receive it. But if we have reached the place where we realize that we must have it, no matter what the price, and are willing to pay the price, we shall never be disappointed.

Is the world still a vast, arid Sahara, without an oasis? Are the hot winds of passion like the breath of a blast furnace, searing and scorching the inner life? Are the waste sands of failure and profitless endeavor like an ocean of flame completely enveloping us? Is there no relief as they glow and quiver? Does there seem no escape? Do the very pores of the soul cry out for water because of the maddening thirst? Then the Man of Galilee will appear and say, "Come unto Me and drink." Will we come today?

### Come to Him to Receive

But notice to whom we are to come—not to the ceremony of drawing the water, not to a doctrine about the water, not to a philosophy concerning the water, not to an orthodoxy of understanding of the water. Those are right and proper and necessary in their place. But they are no substitute for coming to Him. We are to come to Him as the fountain from whom we are to drink; not merely to the preacher, not simply to the baptismal pool or to the church, but to Jesus. For "all the promises of God in Him are yea, and in Him Amen." 2 Cor. 1:20.

What is it to come to Jesus? It is to believe and receive Him for what He offers Himself to be in this verse—a flowing fountain of divine life, love, and satisfaction, and the Holy Spirit as the bearer of those streams of love.

Now, mark that to "drink" is to believe on Him, for "he that believeth on Me shall never thirst." John 6:35. So the incoming and the outflowing of the Holy Spirit are inseparably connected with a new and fuller recognition of, and faith in, Jesus as a person.

And if we so come to Him, He will satisfy the burning thirst. He will bring relief to the burdened mind. He will make light the heavy heart. He will comfort the sorrowing soul. He will give hope to the despondent life. He will give cheer to the downcast spirit, and rest to the weary pilgrim. He will break the chains that shackle. He will emancipate us from the dominion and power of sin. He will solve the problem before us. He will equip us for service. He will put His Spirit within us.

And there is no other way under heaven in which these things can be brought about.

In this last day of the feast, this last-day period in which we live, I ask, Has your heart been satisfied? or is there still a thirst that has not been quenched? Is there still a load that has not been lifted? Is your heart like that empty pitcher, elevated by that officiating priest in mute appeal to High Heaven, a testimony of unfulfilled, unsatisfied spiritual longings? In the Master's stead, I cry today, saying, If any man thirst, let him come unto Him and drink. He that believeth on Him, as the Scripture hath said, from within him shall flow rivers of living water. And I pray that God will bring a message to your heart as we think deeply of the living water.

### Living Water

In this connection the mind inevitably goes to the interview of Christ with the woman of Samaria recorded in John 4:10-14:

"Jesus answered and said unto her, If thou knewest the gift of God, and who it is that saith to thee, Give Me to drink; thou wouldest have asked of Him, and He would have given thee living water.

"The woman saith unto Him, Sir, Thou hast nothing to draw with, and the well is deep: from whence then hast Thou that living water?

"Art Thou greater than our father Jacob, which gave us the well, and drank thereof himself, and his children, and his cattle?

"Jesus answered and said unto her, Whosoever drinketh of this water shall thirst again: but whosoever drinketh of the water that I shall give him shall never thirst; but the water that I shall give him shall be in him a well of water springing up into everlasting life."

Here is affirmed the fact of the provision of the living water, while in chapter 7 the affirmation is turned into a world-wide proclamation and invitation. In chapter 4 of John's Gospel the gift by Him of this living water is the most prominent thought; in chapter 7 He Himself is the gift, the wellspring of eternal life. It is Jehovah's ancient proclamation sounding forth in human flesh, "Ho, every one that thirsteth, come ye to the waters." Isa. 55:1.

Mark that even in chapter 4 the living water is connected with the Holy Spirit in verses 22-24. There are three groups of worshipers: First, the ignorant and blind worshipers, as the Samaritans; second, the intelligent, informed worshipers, as the Jews, but formalists, worshipers of the letter; and third, the spiritual worshipers, not merely intellectual, orthodox, and with outward conformity. These last the Father seeketh to worship Him. He is seeking such today. Are we ready to respond?

But let us return to the living water mentioned in verse 14. From of old, men have sought the water of life. The only real and genuine is here set forth. All others are delusive frauds. But he who drinks this water possesses a "fountain," an artesian well, springing up, or, as the Hebrew puts it, leaping up, from which plentiful streams pour forth, freer than any earthly fountain, never to fail or stagnate. He that drinketh of this water shall "never thirst." How good that is!

I passed through a water famine a number of years ago in a little Western town. The water supply came from a reservoir up in the mountains behind the town, but there had been a drought. No snow had fallen in the winter season, the infilling stream had dwindled to a tiny ribbon, and the water in the reservoir sank to a low level. There was a resultant water famine that menaced the health and welfare of the community. The most rigid economy was enforced to guard the precious fluid. Sometimes in the evening as one would open a faucet, there was but a miserable dribble. The pressure was gone. At other times there was only a sputtering, a tantalizing noise, and scarcely a drop of water would come forth.

What a picture of some Spiritless lives! With the busy toil of the day with its many problems and perplexities, when the living water is supremely needed, it has dwindled to a tiny, insufficient stream; and this is not because the supply is low in the reservoir, but because the channel has become obstructed by worldliness. Oh, the tragedy of it!

But I went to another city where the water supply was from artesian wells that never failed. And there the inhabitants never thirsted, for they constantly availed themselves of the abundant water supply afforded by the never-failing wells.

But while all recognize instantly the imperative need of a constant supply of water for the physical body, many are slow to realize that the spiritual nature is just as dependent upon a living connection with the Fountain of spiritual life. With some the indwelling Spirit has dwindled to a tiny stream with scarcely enough to refresh the soul in times of stress. Such never know what an abundance means, because they do not draw upon the Source. Jesus' provision was that we might have abounding life, as we read in John 10:10: "I am come that they might have life, and that they might have it more abundantly." May God help us to evaluate properly and to avail ourselves constantly of the river of living water which He has given us in Christ Jesus.

In chapter 7 the promise is given that out of the believer "shall flow rivers of living water." But the Scripture also reveals the source—the Holy Spirit who dwells in the believer. The Rock that followed or went *with* ancient Israel (1 Cor. 10:4) is to be within us through the Spirit. The direct personal agency of the Holy Spirit first opens the living waters to the believer, and by His indwelling, perpetually renews the stream so that there is an unfailing flow, yes, even *rivers.*

## An Unlimited Flow Assured

Let us notice that word *rivers.* It implies hugeness, vastness; not a trickling brooklet, a modest stream, nor even a single river, but *rivers,* plural. This denotes constancy, copiousness, and diffusiveness, increasing and deepening and widening. It signifies multiplicity, flowing and overflowing in many directions.

We are to be like the mighty river of Eden. You will remember how it was divided into four heads. The first was Pison, which means extended or spreading; the second, Gihon, meaning impetuous or streaming; the third, Hiddekel, meaning swift flowing; and the fourth Euphrates, which signifies fruitful. As I see what God designs for me to be, and then see my own shriveled, shrunken life, it humbles me completely in the dust. It crushes and lays all the glory of self at the Master's feet.

Yes, and it is to be living water, or, as the Hebrew puts it, running water. It is in motion. So the life is to be filled with plentiful streams of living, running water, imparting blessing and refreshing to others, bearing life and satisfaction and gladness in the midst of abounding death, dissatisfaction, and dreariness. Do others feel a vivifying, fructifying, refreshing influence from your life, flowing in streams from you? In God's provision they may and should. May God search us and reveal our need and our lack, and lead us to the unfailing Source of supply.

Remember, too, the universality of the promise. It includes the weakest and the most obscure in its magnificent sweep. It is for you and me. I ask, Has God verified His promise to us? If not, why not? There must be a cause.

And here is another question: Is there anything

beyond being filled by the Spirit? Can anything that is full become fuller? Yes, so full that it overflows. Thus it becomes a double blessing, first in personal satisfaction for our own needs; and, second, in the grander, more glorious channel of blessing. These rivers of water are to quench the thirsty lives of others, to overflow in abundant outgiving. That is the distinction between filled and fuller—so full that it overflows in streams of blessings.

Again, let us stress, "Out of him shall *flow*"— visible, actual currents. We may not be able to hold much, but here is a word of cheer and comfort: We can overflow a great deal. You may take a tin cup to the faucet, and it can overflow just as truly and as much as a bucket or a tub.

## An Outlet Is Imperative

Every river must have an outlet. Otherwise it ceases to be a river. The inflow depends upon and is gauged by the outflow. I believe profoundly that every redeemed person is a channel through which the Holy Spirit may reach other lives, else he becomes a barrier preventing the Holy Spirit from doing His work. God pity us if because of sin we have become barriers.

The provision is for us to be flowing streams, and we shall be unless the obstruction of sin prevents. Again I ask, Do others see a freshness and freedom, a spontaneity of life and love, in our service? There is no force-pump work or hard labor presented here in John 7, but abounding, irresistible service. It is not a picture of a creaky old pump that has to be primed and coaxed. Its flow is not dependent upon prompting and spurring on. It is not increased by devices, equipment, paraphernalia. It is not developed by pleading, entreating, cajoling.

This flow is not achieved by working up, drumming up, sloganing up. No, it is an artesian flow, spontaneous and irresistible because the Holy Spirit is the spring of the life. It seeks an outlet. Then it is bound to flow. You, reader, may be a channel through which it shall flow. And service on any other basis is a miserable makeshift, an artificial substitute.

By the reference to the flow of rivers of living water, Jesus "spake of the Spirit" which they that believe on Him should receive. I am glad Jesus has made it so plain. Metaphors and figures are sometimes hard to explain. Different individuals often have differing interpretations. But here the Holy Spirit interprets the passage to be the river of His own life that flows through yours and mine. It is the Holy Spirit we need in our lives.

It is the lack of this that is the secret of our spiritual failures. On the other hand, it is this supply that is the secret of every mighty Christian character that has molded the spiritual life of the church since Pentecost. It is this that will prepare the remnant church for her Lord's return.

### The Characteristics of Water

But why does Jesus compare the Holy Spirit to water? Because there are certain processes and characteristics that are strikingly analogous:

First, water *cleanses.* "Then will I sprinkle clean water upon you, and ye shall be clean." Eze. 36:25. It is merely a striking way of setting forth the purifying process of His cleansing from sin, self, and pollution. When we ask for the living water, we are first of all seeking for the cleansing that God alone can do for the soul. Oh, may He do His perfecting, purifying work in us!

Second, water *satisfies.* "As the hart panteth after the water brooks, so panteth my soul after Thee, O God." Ps. 42:1. What water is to the thirsty body, the Holy Spirit is to the thirsty soul. Here alone is eternal satisfaction. As nothing can take the place of the sparkling water, so nothing can take the place of the Holy Spirit. Longing heart, what you need is this proffered living water.

Third, water *revives.* It resuscitates the faint and weary.

"There is hope of a tree, if it be cut down, that it will sprout again, and that the tender branch thereof will not cease. Though the root thereof wax old in the earth, and the stock thereof die in the ground; yet through the scent of water it will bud, and bring forth boughs like a plant." Job 14:7-9.

When a person is faint we bring water. When a

plant is wilted we apply water. Are we drooping trees with dying branches? Has some storm of life broken us down? Has the ax of failure felled the very trunk of our lives? Is the outlook discouraging, or even blank with despair? Here is hope! Through this living water we may sprout and bud and bring forth boughs again. Complete restoration is here promised.

Fourth, water *makes to grow.* Observe these two scriptures:

"I will pour water upon him that is thirsty, and floods upon the dry ground: I will pour My spirit upon thy seed, and My blessing upon thine offspring: and they shall spring up as among the grass, as willows by the water courses." Isa. 44:3, 4.

"The waters made him great, the deep set him up on high with her rivers running round about his plants, and sent out her little rivers unto all the trees of the field. Therefore his height was exalted above all the trees of the field, and his boughs were multiplied, and his branches became long because of the multitude of waters, when he shot forth. All the fowls of heaven made their nests in his boughs, and under his branches did all the beasts of the field bring forth their young, and under his shadow dwelt all great nations. Thus was he fair in his greatness, in the length of his branches: for his root was by great waters." Eze. 31:4-7.

Christians, do we want to grow? Then we must sink the roots of our lives down into the living waters.

John the Baptist was an example of one who grew to greatness in God's sight. Concerning him we read in Luke 1:15: "He shall be great in the sight of the Lord, . . . and he shall be filled with the Holy Ghost." That was the secret of his greatness—being filled with the Holy Spirit. It is still the condition of true greatness.

### The Attributes of Rivers

But speaking specifically of the rivers, they are said, first, to *make fruitful.* "He shall be like a tree planted by the rivers of water, that bringeth forth his fruit in his season; his leaf also shall not wither; and whatsoever he doeth shall prosper." Ps. 1:3. Do you bemoan your fruitlessness? Is your life but a withered tree? Withered trees cannot bear good fruit. We must have water. It takes something more than cultivation, spraying, fertilizing, or pruning to produce fruit. We must have this living water. The secret of fruitage in the life is rootage in the Spirit.

Moreover, rivers *pacify.* "Then had thy peace been as a river." Isa. 48:18. Have you seen the anguish of a soul under the conviction of the Holy Spirit? The same blessed Spirit that first brings conviction of sin to the guilty soul, brings the infinite peace of God when these sins have been cleansed away by His grace. This is the peace we need.

Again, rivers *gladden.* "There is a river, the streams whereof shall make glad the city of God." Ps. 46:4. Oh, the breaking hearts! They are all about

9

us in this world. Sometimes as I talk with individuals and learn of the problems that perplex and the cares that distress, and mark the stain of sin, I can sense to a faint degree the great burden that our Saviour must have carried about as He read people's thoughts, and looked into hearts that were filled with anguish as the result of the curse and blight of sin. But these holy streams gladden the spirit and give the needed comfort and succor to the saddened soul.

Then, too, rivers *embody and furnish power.* In faraway Switzerland there is a famous Alpine glacier, the lower end of which is a sheer perpendicular wall. But the warm winds and the summer sun have hollowed out a great cavern in its mighty side. One can enter the arch and stand in this fantastic cave. But you are chilled with cold, for it is ice above, ice before, ice beneath, ice around—miles and miles and masses and masses of ice.

Yet a crystal stream flows out of the heart of that giant glacier, and begins to journey down the valley. It becomes deep and large, a flowing river into which the birds dip their bills, the herds refresh themselves, and trees slip their roots; and the water wheels of mills and factories are turned by its power. It enters a lake and seems lost for a time, but emerges, crosses France, and turns southward. At its mouth it is broad enough and deep enough for the fishing craft, and even the great ships of the sea, to sail upon its bosom.

How cold we are! How like that glacier! How frozen is our lack of love and fervor, how smug our Laodicean complacency and self-satisfaction! I am appalled at my own coldness in the face of a dying world. May God melt these icy hearts in us, so that His rivers of love, peace, and power can flow through us to the world, as flows the stream from the frigid heart of that Alpine glacier.

### The Source of Infinite Supply

The sole condition is to believe on Him. "This spake He of the Spirit, which they that believe on Him should receive." John 7:39. Shall we not take God at His word? And shall we not do it today? Many years ago a sailing vessel was delayed at sea as it was making for an eastern port of South America. The water was exhausted, and the crew were perishing from thirst. They sighted another vessel. They sent up the signal, "Send us water." Back came the message, "Throw over your buckets and draw." But they responded, "We don't want this salt water to madden our thirst."

Again came the response, "Throw over your buckets and draw." With parched lips and burning throats they made a desperate plea, "For God's sake, send us water; we are perishing." And the answer came back the third time, "Throw over your buckets and draw; you are in the mouth of the Amazon!" For the mouth of the Amazon River is wide enough for a ship to be out of sight of land in midriver, and it carries its fresh water far out into the ocean.

I cannot give you this water, the water of life. You must draw for yourself, by asking Jesus. You must believe and receive His offer. How many are thirsting and crying and perishing for water while there is fresh, sweet water all around them. They are in the Amazon of God's infinite love and grace. How many are crying and longing and dying for the river of living water while in its very midst! It is right here. We have only to believe and meet the conditions. We are to throw over our buckets and draw. "If any man thirst, let him come."

Then he is to have the flowing rivers. What has obstructed the channel, the outflow of the Spirit? I want the channel fully cleared, don't you? I want to be a humble medium for the transmission of life to others. It is my consuming passion to be a simple instrument for the Master's use, to move the hearts of men with heavenly music and bring them to Him.

At the end of old London Bridge one hundred and twenty-five years ago a poor beggar was scraping away wretchedly on an old violin in a futile attempt to solicit pennies from the passers-by. But no one stopped or listened, and his heart went down into his toeless boots. A well-dressed stranger passed, but suddenly halted. Then he returned and listened to the old man, whose weary, wistful eyes searched his face for a trace of charity. But instead of the hoped-for penny, the stranger asked for his violin. He would help him out with a tune, he said.

The stiff, numbed fingers gladly passed over the old instrument. The new hands put it in tune, and began to play a low, plaintive melody. The pedestrians stopped to listen. On the coarsened face of one man a tear stole down, and he dropped a coin into the old upturned hat. And thus with one after another, until a dense crowd thronged the end of London Bridge and stopped the traffic, while the gleam of silver was intermingled with the more somber heap of red coppers at the beggar's feet. Louder and louder, higher and higher, the melody came from the old violin, until it burst forth in a flood of melody such as the angels sing. And the word passed from lip to lip, "It is the hand of the master! It is Paganini playing on the old beggar's violin!"

Oh, I want to respond as did that old violin in the hands of the master, bringing the music of heaven to the hearts of men.

### Invitations of the Spirit

On many pages of the Sacred Volume one finds the calls of God. The Book abounds in them. They begin with Genesis and go clear through to Revelation. But one must go to the last chapter of the last book of the Bible to read God's final appeal and His crowning entreaty to men. Hear it: "The Spirit and the bride say, Come. And let him that heareth say,

Come. And let him that is athirst come. And whosoever will, let him take the water of life freely." Rev. 22:17.

The Spirit says, "Come." Have we a desire to be better, a yearning to be holy, a purpose to be godlike, a resolution to be pure? If so, it was born of the wonderful touch of the divine Spirit. Thank God for His Spirit. It is life to you and me. You may scoff at the church; you may defy God, and crucify the Saviour afresh. But I warn you not to trifle with the Spirit of grace. It is a fearful thing to wound Him and drive Him away, for then one severs the only connecting link between heaven and the soul. I have seen people reject and quench the Spirit until one could almost hear the jar of the gates of mercy as they closed forever on a soul who had done despite to the Spirit of grace.

If in your bosom there is a desire for better things, nurse it, foster it, shield it, pray God to fan the spark into a living flame that will burn on when eternity has supplanted time, and night has been banished by endless day. The Spirit's message is, "Come and drink, and come today."

## The Church Says "Come"

And the bride says, "Come." The bride is the church. Would to God she had always been waiting in robes of white, faithful to the Bridegroom. He went into a far country to "prepare a place" for His bride, and He is coming back soon to take her to her heavenly home. I once read of a young man in an Eastern State who wooed and won a beautiful girl. After the marriage he went out West to take up a homestead and to clear the land and build a little cottage. But he had not been gone long before she began flirting with her former admirers and associating with her husband's enemies. What shall we say of such conduct? I say, Shame on her infidelity to the sacred pledge!

But in a sense is that not a picture of the church, the Lamb's bride? He had not been gone long to prepare her heavenly home when she began flirting with the world, the flesh, and the devil, and intimately associating with His enemies. Is it not time for her to change her conduct and her life completely? Is it not time to order her steps and to keep the eye and the heart's affections single?

There are three things that I know about the church. First, she has made mistakes. I do not believe in minimizing her wrongs, in excusing her mistakes, in covering her indiscretions, or apologizing for her blunders. But, weak and defective as she is, she is the object of God's supreme love on earth. I know, too, that she has within her ranks the best men and women in this old world.

And there is another thing that I know about the church. And that is, she still loves God and loves sinners. No matter what you may have said or done to the church, the church still loves you. If the vilest sinner or the most hardened saint (and they are the hardest of all to reach) should walk down the aisle and yield himself to God, the church would cry out, "Blessed be God! Another sinner has returned to life." And a mighty chorus of angels would catch up the strain, and the echo of the house of God would ring through the vaults of heaven. The message of the church is, "Come and drink, and come today."

Let him that heareth say, "Come." The figure is drawn from the caravan on the desert with water gone and men consumed with thirst and in peril of death. They string out one after the other, just so one can hear the call of the next man. At last the head man sights in the distance a clump of trees, and knows there is water. He turns and calls to the next in line, "Water, come," as he himself presses on. The next man hears, and cries, "Water, come," as he too presses on with speed to slake his own thirst and preserve his life.

All the way from the gates of heaven down to the very portals of hell, God has stretched a line, and with His own lips has started the call, "Water, come." And let him that heareth say, "Come." Have we heard? Then let us every one pass on the blessed word, and press on ourselves. If we have heard the invitation, "Come," let us echo it down the line.

And let him that is athirst come. If the line has been broken, if you cannot hear the call of the church as relayed, or whether you have heard or not, to such God says, If in your soul there is thirst, if in your heart a desire, in your mind a longing, in your being a yearning, the divine call is, "Come and drink, and come today."

### God's Enabling Act

But His supreme appeal is to the will. God places the chief emphasis there. He does not play with our sentiments and emotions. He does not address Himself to our hopes and fears. He appeals to our sense of judgment. He reaches after the reason and the intellect. He addresses Himself to the faculties and the mind. He asks us to choose. He who can create worlds, will not break over the will of the creature. That is the reason why so many remain thirsty, and so many are lost. It is because they will not come and drink. One of the saddest utterances that ever fell from the lips of the Son of God is this, "Ye will not come unto Me, that ye might have life." Oh, the heartbreak of those words! No one need be lost. Jesus tasted death for every man. He is not willing that any should perish. The provision has been made for all. He stands at the door of the will and knocks, saying, "If any man will open the door, I will come in." But the trouble is, so many will not. On this issue our eternal destiny hangs. On this point the battle turns.

Friend, do not trifle with destiny, do not play with eternity. If you perish from thirst, you perish because you will not come. But you say, "I cannot come." Do not miss that little three-letter word, *let*. It is a little word, but it is big with meaning. It is not a permission; it is a command. In the first chapter of the Bible, God said, "Let there be light," and it appeared; "Let there be a firmament," and it was; "Let there be land," and it lifted its head above the waters; "Let there be vegetation," and it was there; "Let there be animals," and they came at His call. The Word of God has not lost its power with the passing of the years. In this last book of inspiration He concludes His final invitation to men with this glorious, omnipotent *"Let."*

Complete surrender through your choice is the only thing that stands between you and coming. God looks upon thirsty souls yearning for the living water that alone can quench the drought of the soul, and says to all the powers of earth and hell, "Let that soul come." He clears the highway. There is no power in the universe that can stop the soul from coming who has made the decision to come. All heaven is back of His promise.

Thank God, the thirsty may drink. There is enough both now and forevermore for all who come, and power is provided for coming: the word *come* is an enabling act. And the power is abiding. This drinking is not merely once for all time. There is continual and unlimited access to Him. There is no need for ever thirsting in the presence of the unlimited supply. Let us come today.

# CHAPTER SIXTEEN

««-««-««-««-««-

# The Baptism With Fire

THERE are three scriptures that form the background for this study. The first is prophetic, or predictive, and was uttered by John the Baptist: "I indeed baptize you with water unto repentance: but He that cometh after me is mightier than I, whose shoes I am not worthy to bear: He shall baptize you with the Holy Ghost, and with *fire*." Matt. 3:11.

The second text is an acknowledgment or confirmation of John's prediction. Christ says of Himself:

"I am come to send *fire* on the earth." Luke 12:49.

The third text refers to the initial fulfillment of this promise at Pentecost, and is the earnest of a larger fulfillment to come before the Second Advent:

"There appeared unto them cloven tongues like as of *fire*, and it sat upon each of them. And they were all filled with the Holy Ghost." Acts 2:3, 4.

For a long time the expression, "He shall baptize you with the Holy Ghost, and with fire," has been burning in my soul. Somehow I cannot get away from that expression, "with fire." From earliest ages the divine fire has been recognized by God's people as the symbol of His transcendent glory, presence, and power.

267

What flaming figures flash through the imagination and cross the hall of memory at the mention of the word! From Eden's gate with its fiery sword, to the burning lamp of Abraham, to Moses' burning bush at Horeb, to the consuming fire that enshrouded Sinai at the giving of the law, to the vivid pillar of fire in the wilderness, to the holy Shekinah that hovered over the tabernacle with its perpetual ministration, to the flash in answer to Elijah's prayer, to the coals of fire of Isaiah's vision, to the glowing symbols of Ezekiel's imagery, to the Pentecostal flame upon the disciples, and finally to the figurative language of the revelator.

We all know what the baptism with water is. We have either seen it or received it. But what is this baptism with fire? It is not something that is in contrast to the baptism of the Holy Spirit. It is not an alternative—an assertion that if you are not baptized with the Holy Spirit, then you must be baptized with fatal fire. The word does not say *"or* with fire," but instead, "with the Holy Ghost, *and* with fire."

It is an explanatory phrase, completing the idea. It is the Scriptural way of repetition to emphasize and enforce a single thought. We are to be baptized with divine fire now to save us from destruction by consuming fire later.

That this is the correct interpretation is attested by these words in *The Desire of Ages,* commenting on this scripture:

"The prophet Isaiah had declared that the Lord would cleanse His people from their iniquities 'by the spirit of judgment, and by the spirit of burning.' The word of the Lord to Israel was, 'I will turn My hand upon thee, and purely purge away thy dross, and take away all thy tin.' To sin, wherever found, 'our God is a consuming fire.' In all who submit to His power, the Spirit of God will consume sin. But if men cling to sin, they become identified with it. Then the glory of God, which destroys sin, must destroy them. . . . At the second advent of Christ, the wicked shall be consumed 'with the Spirit of His mouth,' and destroyed 'with the brightness of His coming.' The light of the glory of God, which imparts life to the righteous, will slay the wicked."—Pages 107, 108.

The meaning is plain when we consider, in the light of what happened at Pentecost, what fire is said in Scripture to do. The reference is unquestionably to the fiery character of the work of the Holy Spirit and His purifying efficacy upon the soul—searching, penetrating, consuming, purifying, energizing the life. When He takes possession of the soul, the effect is similar to the effect of fire in the natural world. For "our God is a consuming fire" (Heb. 12:29), and His Spirit is the "spirit of burning" (Isa. 4:4). The expression, "our God is a consuming fire," is not an angry threat. Rather it is a revelation of His nature, His sanctifying grace and power. Remember, He is *"our* God."

Let us now scan rapidly the things fire is said to do.

### Fire First of All Reveals

"Every man's work shall be made manifest: for the day shall declare it, because it shall be revealed by fire; and the fire shall try every man's work of what sort it is." 1 Cor. 3:13.

We shall not study the exegesis of this text and its primary time of fulfillment, but simply try to catch the one thought—that fire reveals. The baptism with fire reveals a man as he really is. It throws the beams of holy light into the innermost recesses of the soul. It shows us ourselves as God sees us.

When Jesus baptizes a man with the Holy Spirit and with fire, there is revealed an amount of pride, selfishness, suspiciousness, love of position, touchiness, and downright meanness that will be an amazement to him. When God baptizes my soul with fire, I come more and more to abhor myself. I sense increasingly that in me there is no good thing. All I have or am that is worth anything has been imputed and imparted to me from my Lord and Saviour Jesus Christ. It brings me to my knees before God in contrite confession.

And not only that, but it brings me to some of my brethren to tell them of grief over the un-Christlike things in my life—this tongue that speaks so quickly, the suspiciousness of my nature, and a hundred other things. The coming of a baptism with fire will result in a spirit of confession such as we have never known.

Remember the statement by the Spirit of prophecy, depicting the assemblage in the auditorium of the Tabernacle at a General Conference in Battle Creek:

"Prayer was offered, a hymn was sung, and prayer was again offered. Most earnest supplication was made to God. The meeting was marked by the presence of the Holy Spirit. The work went deep, and some present were weeping aloud. One arose from his bowed position, and said that in the past he had not been in union with certain ones, and had felt no love for them, but that now he saw himself as he was. [Fire reveals!] With great solemnity he repeated the message to the Laodicean church. . . .

"The speaker turned to those who had been praying, and said: 'We have something to do. We must confess our sins, and humble our hearts before God.' He made heart-broken confessions, and then stepped up to several of the brethren, one after another, and extended his hand, asking forgiveness. Those to whom he spoke sprang to their feet, making confession and asking forgiveness, and they fell upon one another's necks, weeping. The spirit of confession spread through the entire congregation. It was a Pentecostal season. God's praises were sung, and far into the night, until nearly morning, the work was carried on. . . . No one seemed to be too proud to make heartfelt confession, and those who led in this work were the ones who had influence, but had not before had courage to confess their sins."

Then comes that tragic closing paragraph:

" *'This might have been.* All this the Lord was waiting to do for His people. All heaven was waiting to be gracious.' I thought of where we might have been had thorough work been done at the last General Conference; and an agony of disappointment came over me as I realized that what I had witnessed was not a reality."—*Testimonies,* vol. 8, pp. 104-106.

Shall we not pray for the baptism with fire, which will show us ourselves as we are? We are prone, first, to judge by the outward appearance and conduct, but God looks into the heart. We must have that fire that touches the inmost life, until every sin is disclosed and purged away.

### Fire Then Consumes the Dross

Let us note Ezekiel's striking parable of the boiling pot, symbolic of Jerusalem:

"Then set it empty upon the coals thereof, that the brass of it may be hot, and may burn, and that the filthiness of it may be molten in it, that the scum of it may be consumed." Eze. 24:11.

That is another thing that fire does—it consumes the scum, the dross. But observe this sad comment on Jerusalem of old:

"She hath wearied herself with lies, and her great scum went not forth out of her." Verse 12.

There was no separation between her filthiness and her gold. Mark well the sad judgment that awaits her:

"Thou shalt not be purged from thy filthiness any more, till I have caused My fury to rest upon thee." Verse 13.

We have our choice of letting the purifying fire, the baptism of the Holy Spirit, consume the dross now, or be ourselves consumed in the fierce flames of the last day when He shall "burn up the chaff with unquenchable fire." Matt. 3:12.

Then there is this text:

"He is like a refiner's fire, and like fullers' soap [soap for the outside, fire for within]: and He shall sit as a refiner and purifier of silver: and He shall purify the sons of Levi, and purge them as gold and silver, that they may offer unto the Lord an offering in righteousness." Mal. 3:2, 3.

He "sits" to purify. He is not in a hurry, not impatient. He will bring the fire to the right heat. He will continue it until the process is complete. Yes, our God is a refiner's fire. Let us who are seeking for the righteousness of God, pray for the Holy Spirit; first, to *reveal,* and then to *consume,* that the scum of sin in our lives may be burned out.

> "O fire of God, burn on, burn on,
>     Till all my dross is burned away;
> O fire of God, burn on, burn on,
>     Prepare me for the testing day."

### Fire Purifies Internally

Water cleanses, but not as fire. Fire is pre-eminently the cleansing element. It purifies internally and intrinsically, filling every fiber and particle of matter with its own element. The filth on the outside of the gold, water can remove. But that which is on the inside must be cleansed by fire. A nearsighted man was industriously engaged in washing a window. He rubbed and rubbed, and washed at the window-pane, but he could not get it clean. A friend, passing by, saw the situation, and said to him, "It is dirty on the inside!" That is the trouble with us. We are unclean on the inside, in the heart.

Fire permeates through and through, while the water of our cleansing reaches only the surface. The ore must needs be flung into the furnace, the fires lighted, and powerful drafts played upon it. As the rushing wind fans the flames, tongues of fire leap through the mass, which is brought up to the smelting heat. Then the precious metal will be separated from its stony matrix, the dross parted from the gold. Having dwelt together through the ages, locked in tenacious embrace, they now flee repellantly from each other. Thus the Refiner is enabled to run off the golden stream into the mold of His own designing. Let us pray that God may do just that for us. It is the work of the divine Smelter that we need.

It is the fire of the Holy Spirit that separates the precious from the vile. We cannot get sin out of the heart with the hammer and chisel of our own endeavor. The fire of God alone will do it. When that holy fire burns, it will consume the dross of our pride and vanity; the rags of our self-righteousness will perish, the leaves of empty profession will be consumed; the stubble of our questioning doubts will pass; the sham of unprofitable labor will go; the thorns of our prickly tempers will be taken away; the roots of bitterness, the straw of pretentious unreality, and the refuse of unprofitable talk will be devoured.

All these unlovely things will be consumed by the Spirit of God, until the great Refiner can see His own image reflected in us, as the earthly refiner sees his own face in the glowing metal. We must go through the fire, either now or when He comes as a "consuming fire."

"I will ... refine them as silver is refined, and will try them as gold is tried: they shall call on My name, and I will hear them: I will say, It is My people: and they shall say, The Lord is my God." Zech 13:9.

Fire purifies by consuming. Note these words:

"Then said I, Woe is me! for I am undone; because I am a man of unclean *lips,* and I dwell in the midst of a people of unclean *lips:* for mine eyes have seen the King, the Lord of hosts. Then flew one of the seraphims unto me, having a live coal in his hand, which he had taken with the tongs from off the altar: and he laid it upon my *mouth,* and said, Lo, this hath touched thy *lips;* and thine iniquity is taken away, and thy sin purged." Isa. 6:5-7.

The sin of which Isaiah was conscious was lip sin. And, oh, my sin, too, and the sin of my people is too often lip sin! You will note that in the reference to the translated company of Revelation 14:5, who shall follow the Lamb as His bodyguard through eternity, emphasis is placed upon the mouth: "In their mouth was found no guile." May God cleanse and purify us from lip sin. For there is no member that sins so readily as the tongue.

There is the thoughtless tongue of hasty speech. There is the proud tongue of self-inflation. There is the gossipy tongue of unholy exaggeration, and the unclean tongue of filthy allusion; the unkind tongue of unjust reflection, and the malicious tongue of prejudice and passion. All around us we can see the effect of lip sin. We need to have our lips cauterized, as were Isaiah's.

"Ye shall make it go through the fire, and it shall be clean," we are told in Numbers 31:23. That is the way to be made clean—by the penetrating, consuming, purifying baptism of the "Holy Ghost, and with fire." We need that cleansing by fire to pass over us and through us—to penetrate every fiber of our being, every chamber of the soul. That is what happened at Pentecost. You recall that before Pentecost the disciples were filled with selfish wrangling, striving for the supremacy, seeking for position, striving to exalt self. But after Pentecost self was abased, and Christ alone had first place in thought, in action, and in life. Love, harmony, and the power of unity were seen. They actually became new men.

The baptism with fire does make a new thing under the sun. You put iron ore into the fire, and it will come out pig iron. Put the pig iron through the fiery processes, and it will come out the highest quality of steel. We want God to make a new thing out of us! We want to be cast into the fire, and become the new men and women in Christ Jesus that He designs us to be.

### Fire Frees From Cords of Sin

There is another thing about fire—it frees us. It emancipates; it snaps the cords that bind. In Judges 16:9, speaking of Samson, the Scripture says, "He brake the withs, as a thread of tow is broken when it toucheth the fire."

Sin is binding some men tighter than poor Samson was bound with the cords of the Philistines; but the fire of the Holy Spirit snaps the cords of sin. And it snaps the cords of fear—the haunting fear of men, fear of failure, fear of the world's sneers, fear of the ridicule of friends, fear of loss of position and prestige, in pursuit of the call of God. Think of Peter's craven cowardice before Pentecost, and his holy boldness afterward, in charging the murder of the Son of God upon priests and rulers. (Acts 4:8-13.)

The fire of God not only destroys the fear of man

but implants the fear of God, fitting us for the hour of judgment as called for in the first angel's message; it will separate us from the sins and apostasies of fallen Babylon, of the second message, and it will bind us to the commandments of the third angel's message. It is this that vitalizes the full threefold message.

### Fire Softens and Melts

In Psalms 68:2 we are told of how "wax melteth before the fire," and Isaiah (64:1-3) speaks of the mountains flowing down by consuming fire. Oh, how much we need the melting, softening influence of the Holy Spirit to subdue our hard, harsh, cold spirits, and to fuse us into heart unity with our brethren! This fusing, uniting flame makes us one, even as the volcanic stream rolling down the mountainside fuses into one current everything in its course.

There are mountains of self-will that must be melted now, or we shall at last stand with those who will call for the material mountains to fall upon them and hide them from the face of the coming King. May the Lord melt our hearts, soften our wills, unite our hearts, and subdue all alienation, through the baptism of the "Holy Ghost, and with fire."

### Fire Warms and Banishes Chill

Speaking of fire, Isaiah says, "I am warm, I have seen the fire." Isa. 44:16. You will remember that the morning after the resurrection Jesus stood on the shore of the Sea of Tiberias as the disciples, weary and cold and hungry, approached the land after a night of fruitless toil. He knew they were cold and hungry, and He had prepared for them a fire to banish the chill, and had food in readiness to satisfy their hunger. All about us there are cold and hungry multitudes who need to be fed upon the Word, and to be warmed by the fire of the Holy Spirit. That is the combination needed.

There is a tragic difference between the fire that warms and cheers, and the devouring flame that consumes; between the lightning stroke of destruction, and the power carried in the wires to run factory and streetcar, illuminate home and street, or convey messages by air or wire. Just as wide is this difference between the fire of the Holy Spirit and the flames of fanaticism—"strange fire" of the devil's kindling.

The true is kindled from God above; the false is earthborn, springing out of human emotion. It is stirred by human endeavor, and is aided and abetted by the powers of evil to counterfeit the genuine and so to bring all into disrepute. The true is fed by the fuel of God's Word; the strange fire is sustained by human reason and the revelations of man's own imaginations. The true purifies and sanctifies; the strange fire manifests itself in unhallowed forms of sinful indulgence and unseemly excesses. The true works along sane, rational channels; the false assumes eccentric, abnormal, extravagant lines.

The presence of the false in the world should but summon us to seek most earnestly for the genuine fire of God. The devil is seeking by counterfeits to bring truth into disrepute; but we want, we must have, the fire of God to burn out the dross.

And then we need a ministry and a people that are on fire for God, as other men are on fire for success, money, or distinction. Jesus said, "The zeal of Thine house hath eaten Me up." He was on fire for God. O that we had a thousand Wesleys, Whitefields, Finneys, and Moodys, who would go forth to set the world ablaze with the light of the glory of the final phase of this movement of God among men. The way to set the church on fire is for the ministry to get on fire. May the living, throbbing fire of the Holy Spirit clothe us as it did Elijah and Paul. It will shake this world from one end to the other, and finish the work.

### Fire Illuminates the Night

In Psalms 78:14 we read of how all through the night Israel was led with the "light of fire." Passing through Pittsburgh on a train one night, I saw those great smelters and blast furnaces flaming in the darkness, lighting up the heavens. And as I was thinking along this line, my heart cried out, O Lord, give us luminous Christians, shining for Thee, telling the time of the night as the luminous face of a clock so designed. We need the light of a shining countenance, of a kindling heart, of a beaming hope, of a burning zeal, and a glowing message. All of these will come with the baptism with fire.

And may God deliver us from painted fire, simulated, but false. We want real, genuine, shining fire. It is the fire of the Holy Spirit that will illuminate this final message of God to men and make it glow with an otherwise impossible brightness. It is this that lightens the earth with the glory of God, the last glory that will ever be seen in this darkening world till the Lord of glory appears as a consuming fire to strike down the wicked.

### Fire Makes Permanent

There is another thing about fire: it makes permanent, it inures, it hardens, makes durable. Here is the suggestive text:

"Who among us shall dwell with everlasting burnings," or with the "devouring fire?" Isa. 33:14.

The answer to this question is, Those upon whom the baptism with fire comes now, to burn away the dross. Such will be fitted to dwell eternally with our God, who is "a devouring fire."

Fire *inures.* While there are some things fire burns *out,* there are some things it burns *in.* For instance: Take a porcelain vase in process of construction—beautifully painted with rich colors and covered with a network of gold; exquisite in shape, showing the skill of a master hand. But the slightest touch would destroy its design and ruin its beauty.

The vase must be "fired," or put into the fire, and then the colors will be made permanent, the shape will endure, and the maker's name appear, permanently impressed into it.

In the "firing" process of the Holy Spirit the beautiful colors of the holy life will become permanent and impervious to the attacks of evil. As Paul said, "None of these things move me." Acts 20:24. The onslaughts of evil, the conflicts with the brethren, the persecution of the world, the apostasy in the church did not move him from the fundamental principles of the gospel. He was not moved from the great platform of salvation in Christ only, with its inseparable corollary, the keeping of the commandments of God. He was never disobedient to the heavenly vision.

We, too, must be vessels, inured, hardened, made permanent, having not only the dross burned *out,* but the great sign, seal, or mark of our Maker, and His name, burned *into* the life, that its impress may be retained forever. In time's last hour the Sabbath seal of God and the Holy Spirit are inseparable. Those who contend otherwise must be heralds of a counterfeit fire.

### Fire Energizes Into Action

Fire generates power and motion. The mighty forces of steam and electricity are merely forms of fire. In Psalms 104:4 we read, "Who maketh His angels spirits; His ministers a flaming fire." Is it not proper to ask, Are you a flame of fire for God? I went into a great locomotive shop one day, and as I was being shown through I watched the making of the various parts—wheels, rods, pistons, valves, and all.

Then I saw the assembling of a locomotive in the various stages of construction—part added to part until there came forth the completed engine, weighing scores of tons, and all ready to run. The guide next led me up into the engineer's seat, and told me to sit down. He said, "You may pull the throttle if you wish." So I gripped the throttle and gave it a pull, but not a wheel moved. Why? No fire! Every part of the machine was there, but with no fire in the fire box, no steam in the boiler, there was no motion.

Thank God for the power, the dynamic, the forward movement of this message, especially in the overseas lands. But are we satisfied? We need the outpouring of the latter rain for greater impetus. We need the fire of the Holy Ghost to energize us fully. We need the promised heavenly fire that will speed up this heaven-designed machinery for the full accomplishment of God's work and the rapid finishing of His message on the earth.

That is the power we need. It is vastly more than the power of eloquence or business organization, important as they are. It was the fire of Pentecost that reached 3,000 souls with a single sermon. It is the one thing that will move the hearts of men and the church of God today. Jeremiah speaks of fire burning in the bones: "His word was in mine heart as a burning fire shut up in my bones." Jer. 20:9.

Not all heat is the heat of the Spirit. Sometimes there is the heat of friction, the flame of temper, the fire of passion. God has no dwelling place there. Oh, we must have that Spirit-illuminated Word as a pent-up fire in our bones. That is the divine energy all heaven is waiting to bestow.

### Fire Spreads With Rapidity

Yes, fire spreads, sometimes for evil, as when in 1871 the great Chicago fire in a few hours destroyed more than seventeen thousand buildings, making homeless nearly one hundred thousand people; but again for good, as when in the case of black death or other contagious or infectious disease, it is used to wipe out the plague spots that could not otherwise be rendered innocuous.

As we have seen, in Matthew 3:10-12, fire is used as a symbol of the cleansing, refining power of the Holy Spirit, and in this sense we are thankful that fire does indeed spread; and this fact, I am persuaded, lies back of the expression, "Quench not the Spirit." The word *quench* presupposes the presence of fire, and carries us back to apostolic days:

"There appeared unto them cloven tongues like as of fire, and it sat upon each of them." Acts 2:3.

This was in fulfillment of Acts 1:8:

"Ye shall receive power, after that the Holy Ghost is come upon you: and ye shall be witnesses unto Me both in Jerusalem, and in all Judaea, and in Samaria, and unto the uttermost part of the earth."

The power of the fire of the Holy Spirit is for service and for witness; it purifies and cleanses our lives, thus preparing us to be channels through which the Holy Spirit may flow out in service to others. There is no use in praying for the power of the Holy Spirit for ourselves, merely to consume its blessing upon our own lives. Ah, no! It is given for service. That is the ultimate purpose of the celestial fire. And when this fire of the Holy Spirit comes to us and does not find expression in service, we quench the Holy Spirit. I believe in service with all my soul. But I believe in a service that is set on fire from heaven, and not with common fire.

The apostles needed and received the baptism of the Holy Spirit. Surely it is desirable, needful, imperative, for us today. How can we receive it? Just as the apostles received it—by recognizing our need, by believing it is for us just as they believed it was for them; by earnestly desiring it, and continuing steadfast in prayer; by being wholly surrendered to God's will, by coming into unity, and by expecting it.

One gets the baptism with fire very much as one gets the baptism of water. To be baptized in water, a person must first desire it. He must then go to one qualified to baptize with water, and submit himself, put himself in his hands to be baptized. We must do the same to receive the baptism with fire. There is but one qualified to baptize us with fire. That person is Jesus Himself. It is His exclusive prerogative; He has never delegated it to another. He waits to baptize us with fire. Will we go to Him?

### Fireproofed Against the Day of God

It is said that years ago, in old Dalmatia, the houses were made of bituminous limestone, which is soft, and easily cut and shaped. The whole house was made of it—walls, roof, floor, ceiling—inside and outside. But when it was finished it was uninhabitable, for it reeked with the strong odor of bitumen. The structure was completed by setting it on fire. It burned and burned, like coal, the fire sucking out the bitumen from the pores of the saturated stone, until everything combustible passed away in gas and smoke, and the fire flickered and died out from lack of fuel.

Then the house was finished, and stood, having the appearance of white marble, sweet, clean, and habitable. And if later it was in the midst of a great fire, it would not burn, for there was nothing combustible left to burn. It was fireproof.

We, too, are by nature and by indulgence saturated with the combustible, reeking bitumen of sin. In the coming fires of the last great day all such elements will be consumed in eternal destruction. The only way of escape is to be burned out now by the baptism with fire, and thus be made fireproof, as it were, against that day that shall burn as an oven. So we may become beautiful temples for the eternal indwelling of our God.

In pioneer days, when men camped out on the vast prairies, they would sometimes see a prairie fire coming over the plain, destroying everything in its resistless sweep. They knew that in an hour or so they would be engulfed in the flame. Then they would start a fire and send it to meet the approaching wave, rolling and roaring across the plain. At length the fires would meet, and leap to the heavens in one wild outburst of fury, then expire because of lack of fuel. Thus by fire they were saved from the on-coming fire.

I want just that, don't you? I want to be purified from sin, and to be cleansed from the dross that is in my life. I want to be illuminated with God's full truth, and to be a luminous Christian for Him. I want my cold heart warmed, fired, by His Holy Spirit. I want the energizing power of God in my life, so that wherever I shall go, other men will catch fire, and the heavenly flame will spread.

May the prayer of each of us be, Blessed Lord, do Thou Thy wondrous work in my yielded life. Burn out the lurking sin that lingers. Purify from all the enslavements and pollutions of self. Fill me and fit me with Thine own glowing, glorious presence, and send me forth a flame of fire to illuminate and warm the sin-chilled lives of other men and women.

*Then shall the kingdom of heaven be likened unto ten virgins, which took their lamps, and went forth to meet the bridegroom.*

*And five of them were wise, and five were foolish.*

*They that were foolish took their lamps, and took no oil with them: but the wise took oil in their vessels with their lamps.*

*While the bridegroom tarried, they all slumbered and slept.*

*And at midnight there was a cry made, Behold, the bridegroom cometh; go ye out to meet him.*

*Then all those virgins arose, and trimmed their lamps.*

*And the foolish said unto the wise, Give us of your oil; for our lamps are gone out.*

*But the wise answered, saying, Not so; lest there be not enough for us and you: but go ye rather to them that sell, and buy for yourselves.*

*And while they went to buy, the bridegroom came; and they that were ready went in with him to the marriage: and the door was shut.*

*Afterward came also the other virgins, saying, Lord, Lord, open to us.*

*But he answered and said, Verily I say unto you, I know you not.*

*Watch therefore, for ye know neither the day nor the hour wherein the Son of man cometh.*

# CHAPTER SEVENTEEN

KKK-KKK-KKK-KKK-KKK

# The All-essential Oil

JESUS was still seated with His disciples on the Mount of Olives. He had just given utterance to the marvelous prophecy of the twenty-fourth chapter of Matthew, which holds such a unique place in the affections, beliefs, and teachings of Seventh-day Adventists. And now He launched into the parable of the wise and unwise virgins in chapter 25. It is essential to remember that the twenty-fourth chapter is part of the same discourse as the twenty-fifth, though we do not always think of this, and so fail to connect the two.

The evident purpose of this parable is to enforce the practical spiritual lesson of the preceding prophetic section of the discourse, for Christ did not utter those striking prophecies merely that we might be intellectually informed. A spiritual understanding, therefore, of the parable of the ten virgins is of most vital importance to the remnant church.

Picture if you will that memorable scene: Below, on one side, was the Holy City. At Jesus' feet were the slopes of Olivet and the Garden of Gethsemane. Opposite Him were the desolate hills of Judea, and beyond them the misty line of the mountains of Moab skirting the eastern shore of the Dead Sea.

10

### Eastern Torchlight Procession

The sinking sun had set behind the western hills, and the purple scarf of brief twilight had been flung over the landscape. The golden lamps had been hung in the blue dome above, and earth below was curtained with the shades of night. From their point of vantage the little group saw in the distance an illuminated house where an Eastern wedding with its torchlight procession was in progress. It was customary for Eastern marriages to take place at night, and as in those days there were no lamps in the streets of the cities, each person was supposed to carry his own light.

Among the Jews it was customary for the bridegroom to leave his home in order to bring his bride from the house of her father, perhaps in another village, returning with her to his own home for the wedding feast. With a group of select young men, he started out on this eventful journey after the set of sun, going along through the darkness.

Waiting for his appearance near the home of the bride, was a group of bridesmaids, usually ten in number, who met him with lighted lamps or torches. This nocturnal procession, with its burning, festal lamps, was always one of joyful expectation. And the bride was escorted to the bridegroom's home, where a great feast was in readiness.

Just such a lighted procession was in progress that eventful night of the Master's discourse on the Mount of Olives. As Jesus and the disciples watched, some lamps flickered and went out. Jesus seized upon this familiar and impressive sight as the basis of a solemn spiritual lesson for the remnant church. The waiting bridesmaids did not know the precise hour he would arrive, but they knew he would come that night. While waiting, they lay down because of weariness and drowsiness.

Suddenly, about midnight in the case under observation, the bridegroom was seen coming, to the joy of the prepared, but to the consternation of the unprepared. So Jesus used the incident to illustrate what His coming will mean to those who profess to be looking for His appearing. Consequently, it is the present truth of compelling proportions for the remnant church.

The parable is brief—only thirteen verses. But it is awful in its comprehensiveness. It opens with that arresting adverb of time, "Then." This is the key word to its application. It points to the final consummation. Christ had just been admonishing the disciples to watch and be ready, for "in such an hour as ye think not the Son of man cometh." Matt. 24:44. He had spoken of two classes in the world of waiting servants, the "wise" and the "evil," and how to the latter He will come suddenly, unexpectedly, disastrously. The time of application is therefore just before His Second Advent. Indisputably that is the period referred to. As confirmatory evidence I would submit this clear-cut statement from the writings of Ellen G. White:

"I am often referred to the parable of the ten virgins, five of whom were wise, and five foolish. This parable has been and will be fulfilled to the very letter, for it has a special application to this time, and like the third angel's message, has been fulfilled and will continue to be present truth till the close of time. In the parable, the ten virgins had lamps, but only five of them had the saving oil with which to keep their lamps burning. This represents the condition of the church. The wise and the foolish have their Bibles, and are provided with all the means of grace; but many do not appreciate the fact that they must have the heavenly unction. . . . The name 'foolish virgins' represents the character of those who have not the genuine heart-work wrought by the Spirit of God. The coming of Christ does not change the foolish virgins into wise ones. . . . The state of the church represented by the foolish virgins, is also spoken of as the Laodicean state."—*Review and Herald,* Aug. 19, 1890.

## Oil—the Supreme Test

It is a solemn and acknowledged fact that in the world about there are just two classes: Christians and worldlings, the true and the false, the sheep and the goats, the wheat and the tares, the saved and the lost. But this parable makes a still further division, now among professed Christians. It segregates them as wise and foolish, as prepared and unprepared, as watchful and unwatchful, as prudent and imprudent, as the real and the apparent, the genuine and the counterfeit. And the conclusion is unavoidable that we are and will be in either one class or the other. Christ recognizes only the two. There is no third group. And He has not changed since He gave this parable.

Both groups profess to be waiting for their Lord's return. So they are all Adventists, in the broader sense of the term. There is a prevailing similarity in externals. Both groups are virgins—called to purity, and professing a pure faith. Both have lamps and light and vessels. Both have heard the call. All ten are expecting their Lord to return. All are apparently "waiting," in the night of earth's last hour. For a while no difference is seen by human eyes.

The "lamp" is clearly the Word, for "Thy word is a lamp unto my feet, and a light unto my path." Ps. 119:105. This precious boon is shared in common by the two groups. Both have also the wick of profession. So all are members of the true church, with an illuminating knowledge of Scripture. And how we do need the light of the Scriptures!

The story is told of a man in Carnarvonshire, Wales. Walking one stormy night on the mountain, he was so cold that he put his lantern under his cloak to get its warmth. The moon was shining dimly, and he thought he could trace his way without the lantern.

Suddenly a gust of wind blew aside his cloak and the light revealed that he stood on the edge of a deep slate quarry. In another instant he would have plunged over the precipice. He retraced his steps, and you may be sure he did not again cover his lantern. Thank God for the clear rays of the Word. May they shine brighter and brighter, the darker the night and the more perilous the path.

These ten virgins have all heard and responded to the message on the coming of the Lord, and are essentially correct in doctrine. The two groups are not distinguished as good and bad, but "wise" and "foolish." And Christ says the foolishness of the foolish consisted in their lack of oil. They had their lamps and wicks, but there was insufficient oil. They bore the name, but lacked the one essential qualification for meeting the bridegroom. On the other hand, the wisdom of the wise consisted in having sufficient oil.

The solemn lessons that will unfold as we pursue the meaningful features of this parable, cannot be too seriously considered by the church living at this time. The foolish think the wise are unduly worked up over this question of the oil. Are their lamps not burning brightly? And anyhow the bridegroom will soon come, they reason, and there will be an abundance of oil to last. Even if they should run short, they can easily get more later if necessary. But it is fallacious reasoning. I repeat: Everything aside from this oil is possessed by the foolish. And possession of this alone makes the wise ready, whereas because of its lack the foolish are unready.

### Symbolism of the Oil

By the oil is signified the Holy Spirit. Without the Spirit of God the knowledge of the Word is of no real avail, no matter how orthodox our understanding. One may be familiar with all its commands, its precepts, its promises, and its prophecies; but unless the Holy Spirit makes it actual life, the character is not transformed. The theory is useless without the reality.

We are not to despise or depreciate externals, except as substitutes for internal realities. But the foolish looked at appearances and were deceived thereby. Remember, externals mean nothing with God if unmatched by internal verities. Therein lies the peril. It is not enough to be waiting along with the church, or even within the church. Mere profession is but painted pageantry in which to go to perdition. It is like the plumes and trappings on the black horses of the old hearses of years ago, which conveyed dead men to their graves.

So the decisive test is not that the foolish are without lamp or wick but that they are without sufficient oil. That was the nature of their folly. They had the external equipment, but neglected the heart of it all. They were content with superficialities. They met the requirements as to mechanics, but were lacking in spiritual dynamics. And in some ways that is more tragic than no profession.

The foolish virgins were not hypocrites. They were genuine, and earnest in their way. They were not profane or ungodly. They unquestionably had a sincere regard for the truth. They were attracted to it, but had not addressed themselves to securing this all-essential thing.

How solemn the thought! There may be high profession and orthodox belief. One may have been baptized, may partake regularly of the Lord's supper, may be an officer in the Missionary Volunteer Society, the Sabbath school, or the church; yes, may be an ordained minister, even holding an important official position, and yet be without the Holy Spirit, and thus be among those divinely denominated "foolish," because unprepared, and may be finally lost. The thought that it is possible for *me* to be among the foolish stirs me.

It is awful to have just enough Christianity to deceive the heart, just enough to lull to false security, just enough to prop one up with false confidence, just enough to lose the soul. But thus it was with the foolish virgins who lacked oil. Remember this: Intense Bible study is no substitute for the Holy Spirit; frenzied activity will never compensate for lack of the Spirit; the extremes of sacrifice will not suffice. We must have the heavenly oil, or all is vain. This is Christ's solemn dictum, not mine. The foolish virgins made a fair appearance, but because of lack of oil, they were left outside at last.

The "lamp" used in those ancient wedding processions was attached to the upper end of a wooden staff. It consisted of a vessel, or round receptacle for the oil, into which the wick was inserted, the light being sustained by the oil. Suppose we should say to a lamp, "How do you manage to give out so much beautiful light?" If it were vocal, the lamp would surely respond, "Why, I am not *giving* anything. I am all the time sucking up oil through my thirsty wick. It is the oil that gives the light."

And that is it. Let the dry wick of our profession be immersed in the oil of the Spirit, and we cannot help shining. And only thus can we lighten the world in the time of the loud cry. God wants us to illuminate the night to welcome the Bridegroom. How true and pertinent are the words of the wise man, "Wisdom excelleth folly, as far as light excelleth darkness." Eccl. 2:13.

### Oil Is an Illuminator

How apt is the figure of "oil" as used to symbolize the Holy Spirit. First, oil is an *illuminator*. In eleven Scripture passages oil is connected with light; as, for example, in Exodus 25:6, "oil for the light." You will recall the impressive figure in Zechariah 4: the golden candlestick, with the bowl for oil upon the top, and the seven lamps, and the seven pipes perpetually bearing the oil from the living olive trees for the light of the candles. It was constantly flowing, and ceaselessly imparted. And the symbolic intent is plainly and literally disclosed in verse six, "Not by might, nor by power, but by My spirit, saith the Lord of hosts." There is no mistaking the intent. The Holy Spirit is the source of the light. The Spirit is this oil that we must have.

There must be constancy of supply, else darkness will come. The flow must be unhindered and continuous. It is sin that chokes the pipe line. Brother, sister, is your candlestick connected with the olive trees, so that the supply is unfailing? God does not design that ours shall be an intermittent light, burning low, or going out; it must be bright and full and constant. Remember the solemn warning to the church, "Else I will come . . . and will remove thy candlestick out of his place." Rev. 2:5. That means an inevitable and fatal break in the pipe line, so that the oil ceases to flow and the spiritual light goes out.

God forbid that such a catastrophe should come to any of us. He designs that His remnant people shall both have light for themselves and be an unwavering source of light to others. Of ancient Israel, just before the exodus from Egypt, it is written, "The children of Israel had light in their dwellings" (Ex. 10:23), and this in the midst of the abounding Egyptian darkness that covered the land, typical of the spiritual darkness of today. And it is light that we need—the light of the

Holy Spirit's holiness, love, gentleness, righteousness, and faithfulness. Yes, what we need is "the supply of the Spirit of Jesus Christ." Phil. 1:19.

### Symbol of Consecration and Healing

Again, oil is set forth also as the symbol of *consecration.* Two hundred and two times reference is made in Scripture to the anointing oil. Whatever was anointed therewith was set apart to a holy calling or use. The Mosaic ritual was replete with instruction on this point.

And the anointing oil for the priests and tabernacle reappears in the very name of Christ, which means "the Anointed;" also in His declaration, "The Spirit of the Lord is upon Me, because He hath anointed Me to preach." Luke 4:18. Paul informs us of the nature of that anointing of the Holy Spirit: "God anointed Jesus of Nazareth with the Holy Ghost and with power: who went about doing good, and healing all that were oppressed of the devil; for God was with Him." Acts 10:38. That was the oil.

It will be profitable for us to read briefly concerning the applying of the symbolic anointing oil in ancient times:

"Thou shalt anoint the tabernacle of the congregation therewith, and the ark of the testimony, and the table and all his vessels, and the candlestick and his vessels, and the altar of incense, and the altar of burnt offering with all his vessels, and the laver and his foot. And thou shalt sanctify them, that they may be most holy: whatsoever toucheth them shall be holy. And thou shalt anoint Aaron and his sons, and consecrate them, that they may minister unto Me in the priest's office." Ex. 30:26-30.

The tabernacle and all the articles therein were consecrated, and the priests also. Kings, too, were thus set apart. So we read in 1 Samuel 16:13.

"Then Samuel took the horn of oil, and anointed him in the midst of his brethren: and the Spirit of the Lord came upon David from that day forward."

Mark how it is inseparably connected with the anointing of the Holy Spirit. And Christ's believers are likewise to be priests and kings. (Rev. 1:6; 5:10.) We, too, must first be anointed with the holy oil. Oh, is the oil upon us? "Be filled with the Spirit," is the divine command. "Received ye the Holy Spirit?" is the divine interrogation. And let us not get away from the fact that this anointing was to sanctify them. We read it in Leviticus 8:10-12:

"Moses took the anointing oil, and anointed the tabernacle and all that was therein, and sanctified them. And he sprinkled thereof upon the altar seven times, and anointed the altar and all his vessels, both the laver and his foot, to sanctify them. And he poured of the anointing oil upon Aaron's head, and anointed him, to sanctify him."

In the ancient ritual the head and hands and feet of the cleansed leper, as well as the consecrated priest, were touched with the anointing oil, in symbol of dedication to God. Read it in Leviticus 14:17, 18:

"The rest of the oil that is in his hand shall the priest put upon the tip of the right ear of him that is to be cleansed, and upon the thumb of his right hand, and upon the great toe of his right foot, upon the blood of the trespass offering: and the remnant of the oil that is in the priest's hand he shall pour upon the head of him that is to be cleansed."

But note carefully from the context that the blood was first applied, then the oil. First, cleansing, then consecration—that is the divine order. The head is the seat of thought. It stands for the mind. The hand is a symbol of action and service. The foot indicates the walk of life. We are to "walk in the Spirit," and live "in the Spirit." And there was the anointed ear for obedience. It simply means, "Lord, I will hear for Thee, I will act for Thee, I will walk for Thee." Then the rest of the oil was poured on the head, to run in copious streams over the person. And this oil was bruised or crushed out of the olives. Ah, it took the bruising of Calvary to secure the coming of the Spirit. This we should never forget.

### Prohibition Regarding the Oil

Mark also that there were very definite limitations and prohibitions regarding the use of this oil of consecration:

"Thou shalt speak unto the children of Israel, saying, This shall be an holy anointing oil unto Me throughout your generations. Upon man's flesh shall it not be poured, neither shall ye make any other like it, after the composition of it: it is holy, and it shall be holy unto you. Whosoever compoundeth any like it, or whosoever putteth any of it upon a stranger, shall even be cut off from his people." Ex. 30:31-33.

First, it was not to be used on the flesh. God does not anoint sin. Nor was it to be used on the stranger, those that are without hope and without God. (Eph. 2:12.) No one was to imitate this sacred oil. God abhors the human substitutions of the energy of the flesh, that are but spurious imitations of the anointing of the Holy Spirit. Let us beware of accepting the substitute in our own lives.

This divine oil is called the "oil of gladness." (Ps. 45:7.) It is also the oil of healing. Remember the good Samaritan: he had feet of mercy, for he came; he had eyes of kindness, for he saw; he had a heart of love, for he had compassion; he had hands of helpfulness, for he lifted him; he had self-denial, for he set him on his own beast; he had supporting grace, for he brought him to an inn; and he had gracious forethought, for he provided for his future needs. But first of all he applied the healing oil to the needy man's wounds.

That is also the blessed work of the Holy Spirit. "Such were some of you: but ye are washed, but ye are sanctified, but ye are justified in the name of the Lord Jesus, and by the Spirit of our God." 1 Cor. 6:11. Washed, justified, sanctified! Glorious provision of our God! Such is the oil that the foolish virgins lacked that fatal night—the spirit of illumination, of consecration, of sanctification, of healing.

## Slumber Time of the World

Alas, the pity of it! Because the bridegroom tarried, they all, wise and foolish, "slumbered and slept." Both were faulty—the foolish in false security, the wise in spiritual stupor. Thus the parable emphasizes the effect of the Bridegroom's delay, though it is but the secondary thought. Though He tarry, He will come when they are not expecting or looking for Him. He will not tarry past the appointed time. We have His unqualified promise:

"Behold, the Lord God will come with strong hand, and His arm shall rule for Him: behold, His reward is with Him, and His work before Him." Isa. 40:10.

"The Lord is not slack concerning His promise, as some men count slackness; but is longsuffering to us-ward, not willing that any should perish, but that all should come to repentance. But the day of the Lord will come as a thief in the night." 2 Peter 3:9, 10.

This is the slumber time of the world, when an irresistible desire for repose has fallen upon men. Spiritual relaxation and drowsiness, like an overmastering stupor, have stolen over the world. This sleepiness that has touched the remnant church is not a repudiation of the faith, but rather the relaxation of definite expectation of the speedy approach of Christ's return. It is in the time of waiting that the Advent faith is tried.

Observe that both wise and foolish "slumbered" and "slept." These are different words in the Greek. *Slumbered* means rather that they nodded and became drowsy. It is the initial stage. Doubtless the wise *slumbered*, while the foolish *slept*. The first is a half involuntary lethargy; the second is a conscious, deliberate yielding to it.

It was at midnight, late and dark—that hour of deep sleep and danger of fatal surprise—that the bridegroom came. The delay and slumber and midnight coalesce. Then comes the warning of a faithful sentinel. The cry is raised by someone not asleep, "Behold, the bridegroom cometh; go ye out to meet him." It is sudden and unexpected, but it is heard by all the sleepers, and all are startled from their slumber. Both groups are taken by surprise, and the foolish wholly unawares. It is the authoritative notice of his approach, and all must answer the summons without delay.

When Christ comes we must be prepared to meet Him. The coming of the Lord will be the test of our profession. It is in that crisis that all character and inner experience are revealed.

## The Fatal Oil Shortage

All the virgins are now awake. All trim their lamps, foolish as well as wise. They make all the necessary human preparation possible, and all give forth light. Both look and act the same. The parable is designed to show how up to the very last the unprepared may be confounded with the prepared. But now the real distinction becomes apparent. Not conscious of their real condition, the foolish had a vain confidence in their readiness. But with dismay they suddenly see the flame of their lamps waning and flickering, and they cry, "Our lamps are going out" (verse 8, margin)—and that right at the crucial moment.

It was this that discovered to them their fatal lack. It is not enough that any lamp give forth a gleam today. It must blaze forth during the time of trouble, when we stand without an Intercessor.

Christ within, through the Holy Spirit, is our only hope of glory. This is the most essential truth that we as Seventh-day Adventists have yet to learn. With hearts lulled into security, the foolish did not dream of their danger. They were startled from their lethargy, only to discern their dire destitution. It was a terrible discovery, a tragic awakening. They thought they were all right, but found with unspeakable horror that they were all wrong. And the radical difference was the lack of the oil of the Holy Spirit. The form was there, but the Spirit was lacking. The lamp was there, but the oil was about exhausted. The Bible was still read, and prayer offered; religious movement was still kept up.

There was a name to live—but death! It is like the shriveled body of the Roman guard found in the excavated city of Pompeii, with helmet and armor on, and bony fingers clasping his spear—but dead; or like the ship of death, found floating in the Arctic, with a dead helmsman at the wheel, a dead officer with his log book before him, dead seamen in their bunks—a derelict ship of death.

What should these foolish virgins do? They burst into a fit of tears and rage. In a frenzy they entreat the wise to supply their lack. "For mercy's sake, give us of your oil!" they plead. Too late they see that the oil is the all-essential. Too late they discover their tragic mistake. Yes, the day is coming when the unprepared will frantically seek help from the prepared. The hour is swiftly approaching when some in the church will turn in piteous appeal to those who they now think are excited and extreme.

But it will be utterly vain. Man can give the lamp and the wick. In other words, he can teach the Bible to another; but he cannot give the oil, the Holy Spirit. That is God's prerogative solely. There is no use looking to some friend or preacher for this heavenly gift. Each must go to the same Source. Every phase of salvation is a transaction between the individual soul and God. "None of them can by any means redeem his brother, nor give to God a ransom for him." Ps. 49:7.

And when the wise respond in refusal, in this part of the parable that takes the form of a dialog between the foolish and the wise, it simply means that no one has a superfluous amount which can be transferred to another. As relates to the Holy Spirit, none can supply another's lack. It is simply not transferable. The supply is direct from God to the soul. The reality of possessing the oil cannot be externally transmitted. It must be internally experienced.

The foolish had evidently believed in a community of supply, a common stock that would somehow see them through. But it was a false notion. No one will be swept into the harbor on the crest of a general wave. Some will be as dry as Gideon's fleece, with the dews of the latter rain all about them.

## Must Be Secured in Time

We need oil. We want oil. We must all have oil. We cannot do without it. Had we not better address ourselves now to our greatest need, remembering it is an individual matter? This holy necessity is not transferable, any more than one man can believe for another. "Though Noah, Daniel, and Job, were in it, as I live, saith the Lord God, they shall deliver neither son nor daughter; they shall but deliver their own souls by their righteousness." Eze. 14:20. The wise were not niggardly or selfish. The oil was not theirs to give. And all the lamps would have gone out, had the wise attempted to divide.

The foolish trimmed their wicks. They wanted to buy. They were desperately anxious to repair their irreparable loss. But midnight is a singularly unfit time to obtain what they had omitted to secure in a favorable time. The holy oil may be secured by all, but it must be obtained in time. Through Christ a complete supply may be obtained. He alone is the source. But it was too late when they troubled themselves.

It was their emptiness of spirit that brought the anguish of despondency. Ah, it is the second coming of Christ that will make this internal difference apparent. One group lift up their heads, for their redemption draweth nigh; the other are overwhelmed with unutterable consternation, for it is their undoing.

Where can they get the oil? Not from man, not from the church, not from books, not even from the Bible (I say it reverently), but only from God. And then it was too late! While they frantically try to buy, the wise go in to the feast, and the door is shut—yes, shut for eternity, never again to be opened. The case of these unwise virgins was as hopeless as that of the worldly young woman who turned away from a friend's appeal, saying, "I want only time enough when I die to say just two words, 'Lord, save.'" But having neglected her soul's preparation, she was suddenly called, and her two words were a wail of despair, "Too late, too late."

They that were ready and had oil, went in. Theirs was a readiness that was internal, not external. It was not a mechanical preparation. The foolish did not realize the call would come so suddenly, and that there would be such a little interval before "the door was shut." Dreadful, fateful words! No hope beyond! They knocked, but there was no response. They pleaded, "Master, open to us," but He replied, "I know you not."

Ponder well those words. They are the saddest of all sad words that can ever fall upon the human ear. He had never known them. There had been limited fellowship of Spirit with spirit, but no full abiding of Christ in the heart, no glorious indwelling of the Lord, the Spirit, and they did not know Him. We may know ten thousand things about Jesus, and never know Him. We cannot live without Jesus here and expect to live with Him in heaven.

The foolish virgins were left standing on the chill and empty street in the blackness of eternal night. All their labor was lost, all their preparation was useless, all their watching in the cold, dark hours was of no avail. Outside with the rejecters of God! The pity of it all! Why? *No oil!*

### The Line of Demarcation

There will be many who will demand entrance and claim admission to the heavenly wedding feast on the ground of profession of faith and earnest activity.

But hear the Saviour's words: "When once the master of the house is risen up, and hath shut to the door, and ye begin to stand without, and to knock at the door, saying, Lord, Lord, open unto us; and he shall answer and say unto you, I know you not whence ye are." Luke 13:25. "Not every one that saith unto Me, Lord, Lord, shall enter into the kingdom of heaven; but he that doeth the will of My Father which is in heaven. Many will say to Me in that day, Lord, Lord, have we not prophesied in Thy name? and in Thy name have cast out devils? and in Thy name done many wonderful works? And then I will profess unto them, I never knew you: depart from Me, ye that work iniquity." Matt. 7:21-23.

They say: "Was I not a member of the Seventh-day Adventist Church?" "Did I not do my share in all our glorious campaigns?" "Was I not a teacher in the Sabbath school?" "Did I not sit on the front seat and fervently cry 'Amen'?" Inexpressibly sad the disappointment! And all so needless! Saying, "Lord, Lord," will not open the door; nor will the recital of our good works unlock the portals of the kingdom.

Heaven is a prepared place for prepared people. There is no admission to others. And that preparation will come only to those who submit to the work and filling and constant supply of the Holy Spirit.

This is the midnight of the world. Spiritual darkness as black as the pit has settled down upon the earth. We have already reached the hour foretold by the prophet: "Behold, the darkness shall cover the earth, and gross darkness the people: but the Lord shall arise upon thee." Isa. 60:2. We are now in the slumbering time when the drowsiness of the flesh is joined to the dreadful anesthesia of sin. But it is also the time of the loud cry, centering around the preparation needful to meet the heavenly Bridegroom.

Jesus is coming soon, coming suddenly, speedily, unexpectedly. Are we prepared according to God's specification? How is your lamp today? Is it trimmed and burning bright? Ah, we zealously sing, "O brother, is your lamp trimmed and burning?" That is good, as far as it goes, but it does not go far enough. There may be a flame, and the oil be about exhausted. "O brother, is there oil in your vessel?" That is the song that the remnant church needs to sing. That is the prayer we need to offer.

How about the oil in the lamp vessel? If the line of demarcation were to be drawn today, this hour, this moment, on which side would you be found? It is the most important question in the world. May God in His infinite mercy awaken and arouse us each and all.

Murillo, the great Spanish artist, painted a wonderful picture of a monk in a cell writing. Something significant in the face and attitude of the monk strikes the beholder. He had been writing all his life, but before completing his work, death summoned him. He pleaded to be allowed time to finish his work. He was granted a specified time.

The artist depicts him just after he had seized his pen again and resumed his work. Intensity of feeling is thrown into every line of the wan, ghastly face. His were lips that had talked with death, and eyes that had looked on eternity. Convulsive energy marks his posture as he writes. The "powers of the world to come" had laid hold of his soul. God give to us just such intensity of purpose in seeking for the Holy Spirit. And that there is a very real and growing recognition of need, and a reaching after the provision, is blessedly true.

### Obtain Before Too Late

The counsel of the Master to us today is, "Watch ye therefore," lest through carelessness and worldly conformity we be content with the theory, glide along with the stream until it is too late, and be swept over the falls. True wisdom consists in being always ready according to heaven's program and provisions. And, praise God, there is divine provision for our human infirmity.

We are face to face with eternity. Lord William Russell on his way to the scaffold took out his watch, and handed it to the physician who had attended him. "Will you kindly take my timepiece and keep it? I have no more use for it. I am now dealing with eternity." Time with us is slipping away. Eternity is coming soon. Are we prepared for the change?

A few years ago I went by ship from Portland,

Oregon, to San Francisco. It was a stormy, foggy trip, but we safely reached and entered by the Golden Gate into the San Francisco harbor. Another and following ship, however, hailing from a different port, went down on the rocky coast not far from the desired haven. And the captain was among the missing. I shall never forget the words of the captain's wife, as reported in the newspapers. Instead of the familiar footfall, it was the bearer of the tragic tidings who came to the door of the captain's little cottage. And when she heard, she threw up her hands with the cry, "My God, lost! and so near home! Lost, and so near home!"

Such was the fate of the foolish virgins.

But, thank God, the foolish can still become wise. It is not yet too late. This is God's hour to give transforming grace. Casting aside all figures, God is more willing to give His Holy Spirit to those who ask than to bestow any other gift, for in His train all other blessings flow. And without Him the soul is barren and forlorn. Christ withdrew His localized, physical, bodily presence from the earth, so that He might be universally present in each yielded life through the Holy Spirit. Let us buy of Him the oil in this day of opportunity, and permit Him to dwell in the life as the constant source of supply. Then we shall never know the anguish of despair by being left in darkness while others go in to the feast, and the door is shut.

# THE DIVINE CALL TO PRAYER

ᚲᚲᚲᚲᚲᚲᚲᚲᚲᚲᚲ

"ASK ye of the Lord rain in the time of the latter rain; so the Lord shall make bright clouds, and give them showers of rain, to every one grass in the field." Zech. 10:1.

"Sanctify ye a fast, call a solemn assembly, gather the elders and all the inhabitants of the land into the house of the Lord your God, and cry unto the Lord, Alas for the day! for the day of the Lord is at hand, and as a destruction from the Almighty shall it come." Joel 1:14, 15.

"Blow ye the trumpet in Zion, and sound an alarm in My holy mountain: let all the inhabitants of the land tremble: for the day of the Lord cometh, for it is nigh at hand." "The Lord shall utter His voice before His army: for His camp is very great: for He is strong that executeth His word: for the day of the Lord is great and very terrible; and who can abide it?

"Therefore also now, saith the Lord, turn ye even to Me with all your heart, and with fasting, and with weeping, and with mourning: and rend your heart, and not your garments, and turn unto the Lord your God: for He is gracious and merciful, slow to anger, and of great kindness, and repenteth Him of the evil. Who knoweth if He will return and repent, and leave a blessing behind Him; even a meat offering and a drink offering unto the Lord your God?

"Blow the trumpet in Zion, sanctify a fast, call a solemn assembly: gather the people, sanctify the congregation, assemble the elders, gather the children, and those that suck the breasts: let the bridegroom go forth of his chamber, and the bride out of her closet. Let the priests, the ministers of the Lord, weep between the porch and the altar, and let them say, Spare Thy people, O Lord, and give not Thine heritage to reproach, that the heathen should rule over them: wherefore should they say among the people, Where is their God?

"Then will the Lord be jealous for His land, and pity His people. Yea, the Lord will answer and say unto His people, Behold, I will send you corn, and wine, and oil, and ye shall be satisfied therewith: and I will no more make you a reproach among the heathen."

"Fear not, O land; be glad and rejoice: for the Lord will do great things. Be not afraid, ye beasts of the field: for the pastures of the wilderness do spring, for the tree beareth her fruit, the fig tree and the vine do yield their strength. Be glad then, ye children of Zion, and rejoice in the Lord your God: for He hath given you the former rain moderately, and He will cause to come down for you the rain, the former rain, and the latter rain in the first month. And the floors shall be full of wheat, and the fats shall overflow with wine and oil. And I will restore to you the years that the locust hath eaten, the cankerworm, and the caterpillar, and the palmerworm, My great army which I sent among you. And ye shall eat in plenty, and be satisfied, and praise the name of the Lord your God, that hath dealt wondrously with you: and My people shall never be ashamed. And ye shall know that I am in the midst of Israel, and that I am the Lord your God, and none else: and My people shall never be ashamed.

"And it shall come to pass afterward, that I will pour out My spirit upon all flesh; and your sons and your daughters shall prophesy, your old men shall dream dreams, your young men shall see visions: and also upon the servants and upon the handmaids in those days will I pour out My spirit. And I will shew wonders in the heavens and in the earth, blood, and fire, and pillars of smoke. The sun shall be turned into darkness, and the moon into blood, before the great and the terrible day of the Lord come. And it shall come to pass, that whosoever shall call on the name of the Lord shall be delivered: for in mount Zion and in Jerusalem shall be deliverance, as the Lord hath said, and in the remnant whom the Lord shall call." Joel 2:1, 11-19, 21-32.

# INDEX